Praise for *Cultures of Belonging*

"Whether you are a leader who isn't sure where to start or a practitioner looking to expand your impact, this book will help you take a tangible next step toward a more inclusive future."

—TAYLOR ELYSE MORRISON,
Founder of Inner Workout

"HR and people operations practitioners have been waiting for step-by-step support in building effective DEI programs in their organizations, and this guide is relevant, actionable, and oh so needed. The time for *Cultures of Belonging* is now."

—TIFFANY VOLTZ,
Founder of Wellness from Within Coaching

"A great read for organizations that want to learn what a culture of belonging is, how to strategize, and how to bring all of the concepts to life."

—LATONYA WILKINS,
Bestselling Author of *Leading Below the Surface*

"Alida Miranda-Wolff's generous, thoughtful book conveys the urgency of meeting people where they are if we want to create meaningful change. She offers a realistic roadmap for workplaces to shift toward a true culture of belonging while holding space for the ways in which the journey may not always be a straightforward one. The nuanced approaches, concrete action steps, and clarifying examples she shares make *Cultures of Belonging* a truly invaluable guide for a broad range of organizations."

—EMILY LADAU,
Activist and Author of *Demystifying Disability*

"*Cultures of Belonging* centers the employee experience in the DEIB conversation and reminds us that while intention is important . . . it's the impact of workplace culture on workers that organizations need to understand, accept, and ultimately address."

—SUKARI PINNOCK FITTS,
Program Director of the DEI Executive Certificate Program
at the Georgetown Institute for Tr?

T0054592

"Alida Miranda-Wolff provides a valuable framework for how organizations can seriously approach diversity, equity, inclusion, and belonging. For leaders who believe that the strength of any business is driven by diversity and are willing to do the tough but necessary work, this book walks them through the steps needed to drive real progress."
—DAN FUTRELL,
CEO of the Pat Tillman Foundation

"Now more than ever, leaders need to make 'belonging' central to their organizations, but they need help and guidance on that journey. *Cultures of Belonging* is the blueprint and the roadmap to making change possible."
—COLLEEN D. EGAN,
President and CEO of the Illinois
Science & Technology Coalition

"*Cultures of Belonging* is an indispensable guide written by a true expert in the field. It is the rare book that is profound and practical, thoughtful and actionable. If you want to go beyond talk and make meaningful change in your organization, this book is required reading."
—MICHAEL WINNICK,
Founder and CEO of dscout

ALIDA MIRANDA-WOLFF

CULTURES *of* BELONGING

—— Building ——
Inclusive Organizations
That Last

A Guide to Equitable Leadership

HarperCollins
LEADERSHIP

An Imprint of HarperCollins

Published by HarperCollins Leadership,
an imprint of HarperCollins Focus LLC.

Any internet addresses, phone numbers, or company or product information printed in this book are offered as a resource and are not intended in any way to be or to imply an endorsement by HarperCollins Leadership, nor does HarperCollins Leadership vouch for the existence, content, or services of these sites, phone numbers, companies, or products beyond the life of this book.

Book design by Aubrey Khan, Neuwirth & Associates.
"Sun" icon by Made x Made from the Noun Project.

ISBN 978-1-4002-2948-2 (eBook)
ISBN 978-1-4002-2925-3 (TP)

Library of Congress Control Number: 2021950730

22 23 24 25 26 LSC 10 9 8 7 6 5 4 3 2 1

For those who feel like outsiders,
and all of the people who invite them in.

CONTENTS

PART ONE

READINESS FOR CHANGE

PART TWO

IDEAS INTO ACTION

INTRODUCTION

When people think the same idea
and move in the same direction, that's a cult.
When people think many different ideas
and move in one direction, that's a movement.
—LORETTA ROSS (SISTERSONG)

I have never belonged anywhere.

As a White Hispanic cisgender woman with an invisible disability who has navigated careers in management consulting, manufacturing, venture capital, and entrepreneurship, I have experienced a particular kind of only-ness.

Since I can remember, others have defined my identity as, "You don't count."

In the dominant group, my identities don't hold enough power or privilege. I am culturally Hispanic; femme in appearance, sensibility, and behavior; and willing to name (rather than hide) my chronic illness and physical disabilities.

In the marginalized group, where BIPOC (Black, Indigenous, People of Color), gender nonconforming, and visibly "othered" people come together, my identities hold too much power and privilege. I am White, after all, and much of my difference is invisible.

This sense of lack of belonging has followed me throughout my life. I don't have a hometown or a childhood home to visit. I have lost most of my family to illness or distance. I don't have an easily identifiable or relatable culture.

Belonging is a core human need, one so many of us expect to find at work, where the formation of community is a given, but a sense of healthy community is not. Our organizations can and should see us, welcome us, and value us for all we are.

I want you to take a few main ideas from *Cultures of Belonging: Building Inclusive Organizations That Last:*

- Leaders of organizations and teams are now expected to commit to diversity, equity, inclusion, and belonging, as well as be experts on how to achieve them.
- Belonging is your sense that you are part of something greater than yourself that you value and need and that values and needs you back; it cannot be achieved without factoring in social identity and use and misuse of power.
- Belonging comes from developing context, creating connection, building community, and understanding your relationships to power, how to use your power responsibly, how to share your power, and when and how to redistribute your power.
- Using a set of structures, tools, techniques, processes, and procedures, you can design the conditions for thriving and belonging at work.
- The structural interventions you make must factor in readiness, culture, recruiting, retention, promotion, and protection.
- When you make these interventions, you build a healthier, more sustainable organization that simply runs better while also helping create opportunity, equitable access, and justice for the people who drive it each day.

One of my heroes, the trust researcher and scholar Rachel Botsman, defines trust as "a confident relationship with the unknown."[1] I've learned that when there isn't enough time to make promises and keep them, vulnerability is the only tool that engenders that confidence.

Which is why I'd like to introduce myself. Or rather, introduce my personal stakes when it comes to belonging.

My name is Alida Camille Miranda-Wolff.

"Alida" means angel, and I've spent most of my life dedicated to trying to care for and protect others. "Camille" comes from the artist Camille Claudel, who died in obscurity, mostly because she was a woman in the 1800s.

And then there's my hyphenated last name: "Miranda-Wolff." On good days I feel like the bridge between the two worlds on either side of that hyphen. On bad days I feel like the gap.

The Wolffs are WASPs; daughters and sons of the American Revolution, Episcopalian, East Coast, Ivy League, and conservative. They use words like "honor," "fortitude," "Protestant work ethic," and "bootstraps."

The Mirandas are Cuban refugees who fought with Castro to bring Communism to the island and then spread it for ten years across Eurasia before defecting. They escaped to Spain with nothing but the jewelry hidden in my grandfather's underwear. They are Catholic, liberal, and citizens of the world who have only been American since the 1980s.

I have been forever caught in the middle of these two families. I didn't speak English until I was five. I grew up in eleven different cities. I've heard my mom called racial slurs and understood viscerally that no one would ever say the same about me, her fair-skinned blonde daughter. Like many children of immigrants, I knew the goal was to succeed and make money. I also knew that if I did something my Cuban grandparents disapproved of, I would be called "so American."

Then I went to college and that led me to work in startups, which was foreign to both sides of my family. In startups, I finally came close to feeling a sense of belonging, like I had a place in this world that so often misunderstood me. Except that the whole "being a woman" challenge reared its ugly head, and I always managed to be just on the outside, looking in.

Working in venture capital, I put in eighty-hour weeks and had fainting spells from exhaustion while also being on the receiving end of "You do it to yourself" comments. I wanted to earn my place and prove that I deserved my role. I was a unicorn in venture capital: the first woman hired full-time in my firm, the youngest director nationally by ten years, the only Latina woman in VC in Chicago, and just one of twenty-seven in the entire US.

On the flip side, "You know how women are" asides reminded me to minimize my identity; being asked how old I was in board meetings taught me to deepen my voice and give off a more buttoned-up impression; and downplaying my Hispanic culture seemed necessary in order to avoid embarrassing someone who just made a comment that their teen was denied entrance into college to make room for an "inferior" Latinx student.

I was overworked and uncomfortable. I also didn't think I could quit. I come from a family of refugees who have always emphasized survival above all else. I have been making major life decisions around a paycheck since I was sixteen, and at this point in my life, there were no other models or options for me. So I did what I had learned to do throughout my difficult and chaotic childhood: find a third way.

I made diversity, equity, inclusion, and belonging the fifth unofficial core responsibility of my role as director at my VC firm. In three years, I increased investor diversity by 25 percent, brought our portfolio from 3 percent woman-identified and people-of-color-founded to 20 percent, and saw us honored with the official title of most active investor in the Midwest. Our top three performing companies were led by women and BIPOC.

I made the business case, and our sixty-five portfolio companies came to me with open minds; they wanted to see the same results in their own companies.

GUIDING TENETS

How do you know if my way is the "right" way for your organization—that everything I am sharing will align with your own mission, values, and goals? The first step is to understand the tenets that guide my approach and work, both of which have been heavily influenced by my team members, mentors, clients, and community.

- *The business case exists; what matters is how you take action now.* The term "diversity management" has been around since the 1980s, and the question of integration, including in workplaces, has existed since the days of the first abolitionists. Asking why we should invest in diversity, equity, inclusion, and belonging isn't as important as asking *how* we should we invest. The actions you take must be specific, relevant, and possible in your organization.
- *Diversity, equity, inclusion, and belonging (DEIB) is not organizing or activism.* DEIB activities are rooted in workplaces. Unless the organization itself is in the business of activism there will always be a push and pull in how you spend your time because of the pressure to meet financial, customer, and organizational goals outside of the realm of DEIB.
- *The order of things matters.* When change is introduced into a system too quickly, the system rejects that change. To design interventions that stick, you must accept that DEIB is gradual, incremental work. Start by honestly and openly evaluating where you are and who in your environment makes the rules implicitly and explicitly. This does not mean don't think big, it means ground your big thinking in a practical, realistic plan.
- *First build muscle memory, then worry about transformation.* Changing someone's mind is harder than changing their

behavior. Even if you have a leader who you suspect resists DEIB, ask yourself, "Did you build equity processes and practices this person must participate in daily in order to do their work?" Because if you did, their intentions don't matter so much; the impacts they have on others will be decidedly more positive than before. Plus they will get so used to doing the right thing that, eventually, they may even believe it is the right thing.

- *Resistance can be overcome.* If your colleagues don't believe in justice, equality, equity, and belonging, won't they oppose their proposed structural changes? Of course. Change is hard, and our existing system is ingrained deeply into the parts of ourselves we struggle to understand or control. Fortunately, I have seen the worst kinds of resistance gradually shift when exposed to the right balance of logic, empathy, and authenticity. You just have to trust that people can change.

- *Hope and optimism are the only way forward.* adrienne maree brown says this better than I do: "I have come to believe that facts, guilt, and shame are limited motivation for creating change, even though those are the primary forces we use in organizing work. I suspect that to really transform our society, we will need to make justice one of the most pleasurable experiences we can have."[2] We are often encouraged to lean on the pressure of responsibility to push DEIB forward in our workplaces. We have to learn to forgive, not for the sake of those who create harm, but for ourselves.

Above all else, the underlying idea that holds up all of these tenets is both simple and hard: we must believe in the possibility of a better future and find ways to get there.

BELIEVING IN A BETTER FUTURE

There are moments that fundamentally shape the future of who we become. For me, one of those moments came inside a small conference room where I was interviewing a prospective intern. I was twenty-one, and I had just finished reading Nassim Taleb's *The Black Swan: The Impact of the Highly Improbable*. I hadn't given the dense, economics-driven book much thought, but it popped into my mind after the interviewee told me that I was old, and also that the work I did wasn't important.

I wanted to explain to this prospective intern in a way that he would understand that he was wasting an opportunity. So I drew from Taleb's book, which focuses on negative externalities, but also on positive ones. For example, a positive black swan event is when something beyond your control takes place and benefits you despite the odds. Say you are running five minutes late, which results in you stepping into the same elevator as the CEO of the company you want to work for. Because you're distracted and haven't registered who this person is, you don't think twice about striking up a conversation. Before long, you are the CEO's protégé, and you've skipped over several rungs of the career ladder.

As I tried to explain to the intern that this very moment could be a positive black swan event, he doubled down on his earlier comments by suggesting that I probably landed my VC job through affirmative action, and that based on my job description, he'd rather be interviewing with my more "analytical" (and man-identified) colleague. In that moment, my life revealed itself to me in a totally different color.

In trying to explain positive externalities to this person, I suddenly saw major events in my life not as a series of connected tragedies and traumas, but as opportunities. My car accident led me to change my law focus and pursue startups, showed me my boyfriend really ought to be my life partner, and encouraged me to pursue a creative nonfiction curriculum I had dismissed out of a combination of fear and lack of stories I wanted to tell. I ended up with a successful VC career, a supportive husband, and a side job as a blogger and essayist. Basically, my whole life changed for the better. All I had to do was be prepared to seize upon that opportunity as it came.[3]

Moments after walking the interviewee back to the lobby, it dawned on me that the challenges as an "only of my kind" in my firm could be opportunities to create change. I was in a place where at any moment, a positive black swan event could happen, and in order to be prepared, I was going to have to reshape my environment. That was the day I decided to "do DEIB," even though I had no idea that's what it was called. I vowed to say "yes" to anything that would create an opportunity for me, or someone like me, to thrive.

Over time this philosophy evolved, as did my knowledge of diversity, equity, inclusion, and belonging. But the impetus remained the same, as did the orientation to believe in possibility and see every challenge, obstacle, and experience as an opportunity.

As I evolve my own methods and practices in service of building better long-term strategies for equity, justice, and belonging at work in the future, what I plan to use most from this book are the ten principles you will find at the top of each chapter:

- Principle #1: We have to understand what belonging is in order to foster it in our workplaces.
- Principle #2: Managers and leaders are now expected to be experts and advocates on diversity, equity, inclusion, and belonging.
- Principle #3: Becoming an inclusive organization requires investing in equity early, consistently, and uncompromisingly.
- Principle #4: If you introduce change into a system too quickly, the system will reject that change.

- Principle #5: Too often, our vision, values, and mission exist solely on our walls and our company websites. What matters is that we define them with our employees, and then develop behaviors we can all live by and share in daily, weekly, monthly, quarterly, and annually.
- Principle #6: A DEIB recruiting strategy creates the space for a diverse, equitable, *and* inclusive workforce.
- Principle #7: Onboarding is such a crucial part of the employee experience, especially for marginalized groups, that it deserves its own special category.
- Principle #8: Retention is about anticipating employee needs, especially the needs of those most likely to experience exclusion and face discrimination. Good leaders have an open-door policy; great leaders walk the halls.
- Principle #9: Make promotion paths transparent, information about the process of advancement readily available, and honesty about opportunities and employee performance—or the lack thereof—a standard practice.
- Principle #10: Safety is our most basic human need; belonging, self-actualization, or any higher orders of needs cannot exist unless people feel safe first.

As you build your own long-term strategies for change, whether for yourself, your team, your company, or perhaps even something greater, ask yourself what you can take pleasure in, celebrate, and enjoy. There is power in being able to see the state of things with clear eyes and still choose to move forward.

PART ONE
READINESS FOR CHANGE

How do you measure readiness for change?

You can only measure readiness if you know what it is.

At my DEIB consulting firm, Ethos, readiness refers to how prepared you are for making changes around social identity and DEIB within your organization. This involves understanding your current state in terms of perspectives, emotions, energy, resources, time, and money.

You measure readiness by naming what it would take to make these organizational changes, and then rigorously interviewing, surveying, and observing to see if the organization has what it needs to move forward. This process often results in a spectrum that shifts moment to moment, but nevertheless grounds how you decide to move forward realistically.

In our assessments, we often find discrepancies. For example, when employees report a high commitment to change and a high level of preparation for forward movement, their leaders often report a low commitment and low level of preparation, but also report feeling pressured to do something based on company-wide feedback. Why are there such polar opposite perspectives between employees and corporate leadership in these cases? Because leaders don't have any reason to change for the same reason employees are asking so vocally for it. These leaders aren't the ones impacted by the discrepancies. They don't feel the pain points.

Similarly, respondents in companies may report a high commitment to change, but because of profitability challenges and external stakeholders, a low level of resources to mobilize (in other words, they aren't sure they can afford it).

It's our philosophy that all of this can be worked through; the data lets us know the scope and scale we can pursue. We need readiness to understand what change we can introduce into the system that the system will accept.

WHAT IT MEANS TO BELONG

To belong is to matter.

—ROY BAUMEISTER

──────── PRINCIPLE #1 ────────

We have to understand what belonging is
in order to foster it in our workplaces.

I spend a lot of time observing and understanding ideological divisions. Command-and-control leadership versus servant leadership. Work-life balance versus work-life integration. Privacy versus authenticity. Radical candor versus diplomacy. Top-down decision-making versus consensus-based agreements. Color blindness versus reparations.

What's interesting to me is that the word "belonging" doesn't conjure the same divides. Virtually everyone I talk to either directly or indirectly seeks it, wants it, and believes in the value of it.

The desire of the separated to become part of the whole, and become more whole in the process, shows up in organizations and institutions across disciplines, whether it's religion, activism, community service, or work. But as much as people at work believe in the importance and power of belonging, they don't all agree on whether it should be fostered by the organization or the employees.

BELONGING AT WORK

At the beginning of 2019, I had the opportunity to bring a long-standing dream to life. Through a partnership with the Illinois Technology Association, I was designing a new program called the Women Influence Chicago (WIC) Accelerator. The idea was simple: invest in woman-identified leaders in technology to close a major gap.

In the city of Chicago there were fewer than twenty woman-identified Chief Technology Officers despite a pool of thousands of growth-stage technology companies. In our analysis of the current gender equity–focused programs and initiatives in the city, we found that the most junior level technical employees and most senior level leaders had access to ample support. However, there was almost nothing in place for mid-career technologists who were at a critical turning point in their careers.

According to "tech leaver" research conducted by the Kapor Center, 40 percent of those who permanently leave the technology industry cite unfairness at work. Of that 40 percent, women and BIPOC made up the majority. One in ten women had received unwanted sexual attention, 30 percent of underrepresented women of color were passed over for a promotion, and 27 percent of women left due to dissatisfaction with their work environments.[1]

Meanwhile at Ethos we were working doggedly on helping transform work environments, especially to eliminate gender-based harassment and microaggressions. I shared the Illinois Technology Association's view that we could help those on the cusp of leaving potentially fulfilling and lucrative careers in technology by providing them with the self-advocacy tools and leadership coaching we knew they weren't getting inside of their companies. By equipping the most underrepresented midcareer women—those in technical roles—and specifically investing in women of color, we could offer the support they weren't getting from their companies.

I embarked on a two-month research mission, interviewing twenty woman-identified engineers, UX/UI designers, data scientists, and technical product managers. What I heard over and over again was:

- "I need to be better at advocacy. I tend to fall back into inquiry, but as I advance more, I need to be better at advocating for something. I need the conviction that, 'This is the right thing to do.'"
- "I don't have a good mentor right now. I have people I can go to for advice, but not one relationship where someone can tell me my strengths and weaknesses. So having more of a mentor or even a sponsor relationship is one thing I need to work on."
- "When it comes to my career path, to be honest, I am lost. Should I read a book? Should I go to a training? Which one?"
- "I have more of a confidence issue. I know the information, but it's about speaking up. That's a personal thing of mine. My manager said to get to the senior level I need to take more ownership and speak up in meetings."

These women didn't need technical training; they needed guidance, mentorship, and leadership skills.

With this feedback in mind, along with the Women Influence Chicago Advisory Board and program staff, I designed a four-month program made up of four workshops ranging in topics from self-advocacy and effective communication to managing teams and negotiation. Each workshop was followed by a facilitated forum where peers came together with a facilitator to talk through how they applied what they learned and where they had successes versus challenges. Participants also had Super Mentors who had gotten to the C-suite in technical roles, and a designated career coach focused on steering their growth.

In our first program, we had seventeen participants, fifteen of whom were promoted by their graduation. This exceeded our own wildest expectations, so we asked the graduates: How did this happen?

Our board members theorized that networking with mentors and learning critical leadership skills primed them for success (which I don't dispute), but the participants didn't mention this at all. Three words came up for them: Community. Support. Belonging.

The response resonated with me for two reasons. First, I taught their initial workshop, led their monthly forum, coached half of the cohort, and managed our mentors; I could see that something unique and different was happening in the ways they connected with one another more than in the concrete skills they were learning. They had even named themselves "Wiccans" and called the one man-identified member of the staff "Warlock." I was trying to help them achieve their promotions through learning initiatives; but they were able to achieve their success because they were part of a greater community.

Second, early on in my career I'd had my own tech-leaving experience. I had been promoted to a head of communications role at an early-stage startup where I was surrounded by engineers. I felt disconnected from the team as the only woman, the only communicator, and the only non-engineer. In an effort to feel a greater sense of connection and belonging (not to mention seeing the potential job prospects), I quietly started teaching myself to code. Eventually I shared with my manager that I thought coding might be a future career path for me, and I wanted to try some in the organization. His response was: "Why would you do that? As a woman, you are a natural communicator. Why would you go against your nature? People like me are engineers."

I was twenty, with no peers and no community. I'd never had a mentor and I certainly didn't have a sounding board. I took his word at face value.

But what if I'd had a community? What if I'd felt a sense of belonging in a place that made me feel valued, deserving, and *ready* to make this kind of change?

That's what WIC was for our participants. The ideas in the program weren't new to them; the support system and social environment was. When I asked one director of product who had started the cohort as a product manager why she decided to push for her promotion again after being turned down before the program, she said, "Because everyone encouraged me. And I thought, being part of this program means I have a responsibility to advocate for myself. I owe it to myself and to everyone else here."

When we designed a program that gave woman-identified midcareer technologists what they were missing in their workplaces, we ended up creating the structure for a culture of belonging.

UNDERSTANDING CULTURE AND BELONGING

Culture and belonging are not the same, though they are often talked about interchangeably. To start, not all cultures are healthy, inclusive, supportive, or positive. Similarly, even in healthy cultures, not everyone will feel a sense of belonging. In fact, that's to be expected and isn't necessarily wrong.

To make sense of what "cultures of belonging" are, we have to start with some basic definitions.

Culture on its own is simply a shared way of life. It's neutral in nature. I'm betting you've seen clear examples of unhealthy, healthy, good, and bad ones in your career. The best definition of a *healthy* culture I have seen comes from historian and scholar Joshua Rothman. He defines culture as happening when "a group of people might discover, together, a good way of life; that their good way of life might express itself in their habits, institutions, and activities; and that those, in turn, might help individuals flourish in their own ways."[2] For Rothman, culture is not just a shared way of life or a set of behaviors or values. It's an intentional process that people in a group engage in together. Importantly, in his definition, culture doesn't automatically equate to belonging either.

Belonging is your sense that you are part of something greater than yourself that you value and need and that values and needs you back. In other words, belonging creates a strong sense of connection, reciprocity, and shared value. No matter how hard you try, not every employee will value your organization or feel they are part of it in a meaningful way. Employees may disagree with your goals or your values; they may lose touch with your mission and have a desire to branch out into other opportunities as a result. What matters is that you are creating a culture where everyone *could* feel belonging because they have the access and ability to participate in the organization's structures, growth, ideals, and principles, and they are shown that they are appreciated and valued through a wide range of cues (ones we will explore in the following chapters).

A *culture of belonging*, then, is one built on access, reciprocity, and sharing of power and opportunity. It is not a culture that excludes anyone on the basis of social identity, though it might set clear parameters around employee orientations, motivations, and aspirations.

Let me give you an example. In building Ethos, I have been obsessed with creating a culture of belonging, and so far, based on employee responses, I've mostly succeeded. With the exception of one person. A Latinx, man-identified former employee on my team said he felt he did not belong, despite the fact that members of the team routinely reached out, spent time with him, welcomed his ideas, and encouraged his professional development. When I asked him why he felt excluded, he shared that his vision for the company was that we remained small, didn't hire any new people, and avoided productization in favor of greater customization. He felt "on the outs" in terms of what he wanted and what the rest of the team, including me, wanted.

A culture of belonging is *not* one where I would have worked with the team to accommodate his vision. Instead, it's the kind of culture where we all made sure we were being inclusive, welcoming, and supportive of him by giving him a platform to share his ideas, engage in healthy dissent, and make his own decisions around his desire to be part of the organization. It was also one where we went out of our way to ensure that his feelings of exclusion were not tied to how we interacted with his social identities, namely being Latinx and one of only two men on the team.

So, why does fostering a culture of belonging matter?

Culture is a process of translating ideas into behaviors, working as a *disseminator* or *transmitter* rather than just an outcome itself. Culture doesn't guarantee equitable outcomes or widespread belonging. A healthy culture that focuses on DEIB, though, is a different story. In this story, belonging is possible for everyone, not just those who "fit" into a certain group definition or paradigm.

But, let's think about a culture of belonging in practical terms. In that Kapor study, two-thirds of respondents said they would have stayed at their organization if it had "fixed its culture." The study also found that just having a diversity, equity, inclusion, and belonging strategy resulted in lower rates of people leaving due to unfairness. Interestingly, the study, which looks at unfairness and social identity, treats diversity, equity, inclusion, belonging, and culture as interrelated rather than separate concepts.

For years, our clients at Ethos told us they had to get their culture right or "fix their culture" and *then* focus on DEIB. This attitude was so entrenched that we used to call ourselves a culture consulting firm with a DEIB focus just so that organizations would start making investments in DEIB sooner rather than later. Part of this came from the internal pressures they were facing around culture anyway, apart from concerns over social identity or belonging. Since so many businesses still readily accept the business case for culture over the ones for diversity, equity, inclusion, and belonging, there is less resistance to approaching the former first.

The first argument in the case for investing in cultivating a healthy culture is that it's the single biggest driver of employee performance. As Simon Sinek details in *Leaders Eat Last: Why Some Teams Pull Together and Others Don't*, our performance in groups is tied to how safe we feel. If we feel safe in our environments and among our peers and leaders, we can unleash our full potential because we aren't spending mental energy or crucial time navigating complicated relationships or protecting ourselves.[3] Also, research shows us that we work harder for people we care about; if we feel committed to our teammates and our company's vision, we are more likely to push through hard times, excel in good times, and strive for excellence across the board.[4]

It's human to overperform when we feel believed in and like we belong. In 1963 Robert Rosenthal and Lenore Jacobson demonstrated this principle when they administered a General Ability Test at a South San Francisco elementary school. They told teachers this test would inform them which of their students were academic bloomers (who would demonstrate increased academic abilities later in the year). The test results were given to teachers, and by the end of the year, they proved right. Students who didn't necessarily show academic promise at the beginning of the year were now top performers with higher IQs. Except the General Ability Test results weren't real. Indeed, teachers had given these students more attention, support, and encouragement throughout the year. This phenomenon, known as the Pygmalion Effect, explains why, when we set high expectations for someone and give them the tools to meet those expectations, we see major results. In healthy cultures, attention, support, encouragement, and belief are baked into the fabric of the organization, which triggers higher performance.

The second argument for fostering a healthy culture is that we still live in a world where businesses are powered by people, which means without them, we cannot achieve growth. Since culture determines how employees perform, it also informs the conditions for growth. And growth looks different as a company scales.

As Molly Graham, former COO of Quip observed, head count profoundly impacts the intersection between culture, performance, and growth. In a company with fewer than thirty people, the group dynamics resemble a family's. Everyone knows their teammates well enough to develop relationships organically, walk up to one another and ask questions, and solve problems one-on-one. This is why in smaller companies culture is often taken for granted as "organic" or addressed as an afterthought. There simply isn't as much of a need for formalized culture because everyone is accessible.[5]

From fifty to 200 employees, the story changes. The tight-knit family transforms into a community where the focus is less on the small group and more on the future of that community, the clearly defined roles and responsibilities of its members, and the infrastructure necessary to foster clarity, alignment, and purpose among individuals who no longer know every person's name. Scaling from 200 to 1,000 employees marks the transition from a community to an organization. Organizations are by nature more institutional, professionalized, and formal, which leads to a dramatic change in the tone of relationships, not to mention a need to specialize by role. It's at this phase where employees feel more committed to their teams or departments than the company at large. If culture isn't prioritized, the company splinters off into decentralized working groups all striving toward different goals that aren't necessarily tied to an overall vision.

A healthy culture is one that is constantly diagnosing its stage of growth, setting expectations around behaviors at each stage, and reinforcing clarity and purpose so that everyone can work toward mutual goals according to a shared set of values and principles. Without this base, companies begin to break as they scale. Going from the family to community phase results in misguided hiring and firing, operational systems failures, and duplicative work. The community to organization transition sees top performers leave as they feel unclear about their future career paths; product failures based on the failure of teams to communicate and cross-collaborate; and a shift away from agility and speed as more and more people navigate who is meant to do what. Fixing these breakages slows down growth and company performance, redirecting invaluable time away from bigger goals to an ongoing list of daily people problems.

The third reason company culture matters in a business is profitability. A strong culture increases net income 765 percent over ten years.[6]

Attrition is expensive. When an employee leaves, it costs anywhere from 20 percent to 50 percent of their annual salary to recruit someone new, a figure that doesn't include lost productivity during the time it takes to replace them or the fact that when one person leaves, it usually encourages others to do the same. This doesn't even account for your "key" employees; losing them could cost up to 90 percent to 200 percent of their annual salary, according to PayScale's "Managing Employee Turnover."[7]

Then there's the question of productivity. Employees who are engaged are more productive. Time is a major contributor too. In the first six months of an employee's lifecycle, they are still onboarding. In fact, they don't typically hit peak productivity in a role until two years into a company, which is when they have developed company-specific skills, built foundational relationships, and formed a strong commitment to the organization's future as opposed to just their own. However, in our changing work landscape, the average tenure at companies like Google, Facebook, Airbnb, and Uber is between one and two years. That means employees are never getting to their full productivity potential, compromising profitability.

UNDERSTANDING DIVERSITY, EQUITY, AND INCLUSION

To create a diverse, equitable, and inclusive culture that fosters workplace belonging, hiring people who add variety and diversity to your company is important. However, it's also important to remember that if you invite those people to join your organization you have a responsibility to make sure each person feels welcomed and valued because of what they bring with them. Without that inclusion they will feel like outsiders, tokens,[8] or worse, and they will leave, become dissatisfied and disengaged, or both.

DEIB is part of the current cultural zeitgeist, which means that everyone thinks they know what it is, but a sense of shared awareness is rare to find in workplaces. We can't actually build diverse, equitable, inclusive organizations if we don't know what that means. The first step in creating an equitable culture of belonging is making sure everyone understands key terms.

DIVERSITY

At its most basic, diversity simply means variety, and it's specific to the composition of a group. A person cannot be "diverse" by this definition. While I agree that we all contain multitudes in our own ways, a group can be diverse, but a person is a person.

One way to illustrate the concept of diversity more clearly is to think in terms of biodiversity. Ecosystems thrive when there is a collection of many different kinds of organisms.

For example, in Central Europe, there are a number of beech forests. In the region, the rise of industrialization in the eighteenth and nineteenth centuries led to massive deforestation. Consequently, most of the forests today are young and new. Beeches grow very tall, very fast, which makes them an appealing choice for reforestation. In all-beech forests, the minute a beech-specific disease hits, the trees don't just die, the whole forest does. However, if you plant other trees along with the beeches, like oaks and spruces, when beech disease strikes, the forest lives and the seeds left by the now deceased beeches have a chance to grow again.

Diversity prevents risk and promotes growth.

This general concept applies to work too. At work, diversity means the presence of difference within our contained environments. When we have diversity within our workplaces, we avoid gaps in our knowledge and perspectives that could lead to major company issues.

Diversity at work isn't just about preventing risk, but also promoting opportunity. Innovation at its core is very simple: it's about taking an idea from over here and one from over there and putting them together to create something totally new. When we have diverse teams, drawing ideas from disparate sources and putting them together becomes much easier because we have so many different experiences, backgrounds, and perspectives from which to draw.

INCLUSION

Inclusion allows individuals with different identities to feel they belong within the group because they are valued, relied upon, welcomed, and empowered. This may be on a team, in the general workplace, or in the industry.

Think about inclusion like connection. When we are part of inclusive environments, we feel positively connected to the people around us. What makes inclusion tricky is that it changes depending on the groups we participate in.

You may feel included in your team, but not in your company or industry. When I worked in industrial manufacturing, I felt included in my team. I could honestly share experiences with my director, eat lunch with my podmates without wondering if I should sit alone, and almost never thought about the fact that I was a woman in an industry dominated by men. Then I went to a tradeshow where every other vendor called me "little lady" and women in gold spandex danced on stages with the intent to sell power tools. I certainly didn't feel included in my industry, even though my team worked hard to make sure I felt included when I was with them.

EQUITY

Equity is the relationship between power and fairness. Power on its own isn't intrinsically good or bad. It's simply either the ability to do what you want to do or make someone else do what you want them to do. The problem with power is that it's not equally distributed. Instead, some groups systematically experience advantages while others experience disadvantages.

Equity is often confused with equality. Very simply put, equality means everyone receives the same treatment and access; equity means people get the treatment they need, and the access is tailored to meet them where they are. Unlike diversity and inclusion, which are outcomes you can clearly see and measure, equity is a process to get to those outcomes.

There's an illustration that perfectly demonstrates the differences between equality and equity (see Figure 1). In the top half, a person sitting in a wheelchair, two adults with different body types, and a child are all given the same bicycle. The person sitting in the wheelchair sits beside the bicycle, the larger adult crouches uncomfortably over the too-small bike, the child strains to reach the pedals, and the smaller adult comfortably moves along. In the bottom half, everyone has a bicycle that suits their needs: a recumbent bicycle with hand pedals, a larger bike, and a child's bike give the previously underserved the opportunity to move freely and comfortably. The order of things matters when it comes to equality and equity. We have to start with everyone getting the same access, and then enhance that access by addressing individual need. Otherwise, equity can easily become a "separate but equal" situation where bias and discrimination are cloaked in the language of justice and fairness.

Equality

Equity

©2017 Robert Woods Johnson Foundation

FIGURE I

BELONGING AND SOCIAL IDENTITY

If to belong is to matter, then who belongs really matters. The language of belonging is often generalized to include all people, when the reality is that some people have a much better chance at belonging than others depending on a combination of factors ranging from identity and power to the ways they interact in a system.

WHO ARE YOU?

For many of us, when we think of identity, we default to personal or individual identity, which is who we believe ourselves to be on the inside. Personal identity hinges on our lived experiences, our preferences, and our achievements. But personal identity isn't our only identity.

Cultural identity refers to who we are and how we show up in the world based on our family's customs and traditions, as well as how the places we've lived have influenced us. Personal identity and cultural identity often overlap; our preferences and experiences are shaped by our culture, and our responses to cultural tradition are impacted by our personal identity.

Social identity is a social construct (see Figure 2). It exists to classify and categorize people based on their relationships to power, specifically their differences. Social identity is applied to us by others, and then we may internalize it. For example, as a child I didn't think about my gender identity until I internalized from others that I was a girl. I have a colleague who never knew he was Black until he was eight years old and a classmate told him he was. However, once we have been labeled, we may adopt these labels as our own. Elements of our social identities then become part of our personal identities.

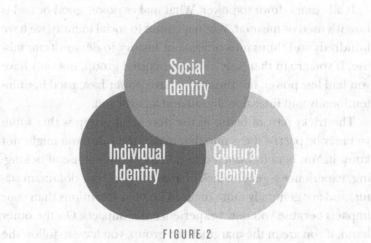

FIGURE 2

UNPACKING POWER AND SOCIAL IDENTITY

Depending on your social identity, you can be "in" or "out," visible or invisible. There is a straightforward way to understand how your own social identity impacts you. Whether you're thinking of government or company leadership, ask yourself: Who makes the rules and do we share in the same identities?

One facilitator at Ethos, Trevor Jenkins, frames this question in terms of the US presidency. Would your social identity help or hurt you in an election? If you identify as a man, for example, it will help, considering that all forty-six of our presidents have also identified as men. Identifying as any gender other than man would detract. You might apply this logic to the industry that you are in. The 2019 Lee & Low Books Diversity Baseline Survey of the publishing industry found that 11 percent of respondents identify as a person with a disability, and 89 percent identify as nondisabled. Of the categories studied (race/ethnicity, gender, sexual orientation, and disability) this is the biggest gap.[9] So depending on whether you are not disabled or disabled, you could determine whether you are in the dominant or marginalized group.

It all comes down to power. What makes power good or bad is how it's used or misused. When it comes to social identity, we have hundreds and thousands of years of history to demonstrate misuse. If you are in that "out" or marginalized group, not only have you had less power, but those who have power have used it, unintentionally and intentionally, on and against you.

The tricky part of being in the dominant group is that while you may be part of the group that makes the rules, you might not know it. You benefit from a natural and organic sense of belonging, experience a general lack of awareness of your dominant status, and are generally more focused on your intentions than your impacts because you don't experience the impacts. On the other hand, if you are in the marginalized group, you have to follow the dominant group's rules and therefore may experience a strong sense of your outsider status.

The incredible work of Amber Mayes and Sukari Pinnock Fitts highlights this idea. In their social identity wheel exercise (see Figure 3), they ask individuals to reflect on whether they are in the dominant group or marginalized group for each of ten identities, and how much time they spend thinking about each one.[10]

Start by reading through each social identity and determine whether you are in the dominant or marginalized group. If you feel stuck on a category, read the social identity table underneath the wheel to help collect more information.

After you have completed this step, go back through each identity and reflect on how often you think about having this identity. Treat 25 percent as "almost never" and 100 percent as "always."

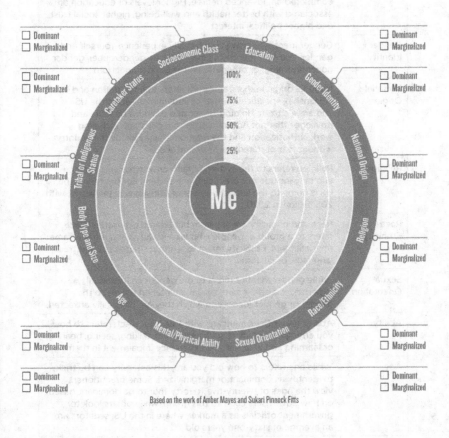

Based on the work of Amber Mayes and Sukari Pinnock Fitts

FIGURE 3

SOCIAL IDENTITY KEY[11]	
Caretaker Status	Caretakers in our framework are people who take care of their dependents as a primary caregiver who is also unpaid. This may involve being a parent or a caregiver to an ill or disabled partner, family member, loved one, or other close person.
Socio-economic Status	Your socioeconomic status is sometimes also referred to as your class and directly relates to your household income. For reference, the median household income in 2019 was $68,703 according to the US Census.
Education	This refers to the level of education you have completed. Answers include some high school, high school graduate, some college, college graduate, began postgraduate studies, or completed an advanced degree. Higher levels of education are associated with better health and well-being, higher social trust, and higher political interest.[12]
Gender Identity	Gender identity is how you internally experience yourself and gender. You may identify as man, woman, genderqueer, gender nonconforming, or otherwise on the gender spectrum.
National Origin	National origin in this framework refers to immigration and citizenship, specifically whether you immigrated to the US and are a citizen. Holding citizenship provides benefits and privileges that not holding citizenship does not, including work authorization and the freedom to stay inside the country without fear of detention or deportation.
Religion	Religion refers to the system of faith or worship you practice and may include *not* practicing any system. For reference, the US is home to the largest number of Christians in the world, with 205 million in 2020.
Race/ Ethnicity	Race and ethnicity are separate but related categories. Race refers to a group of people who are viewed as sharing the same physical traits. Ethnicity refers to a group sharing cultural traits, language, or customs.
Sexual Orientation	While gender identity refers to the gender an individual experiences as their own, sexual orientation relates to the gender or gender identity to which they are physically attracted.
Ability	Ability, under the Americans with Disabilities Act, refers to how you engage in activities such as walking, talking, seeing, hearing, or learning and whether you experience impairment in them.
Age	While age refers to how old you are, this category can be tricky to identify as dominant or marginalized. Some practitioners view the ages of twenty-five to forty-four to be dominant based on how advertisers cater to this group, while others look to government officials as a marker, where in the US, senators are an average of sixty-one years old.

SOCIAL IDENTITY KEY[11]	
Body Type and Size	Body type and size refers to the physical characteristics of your body, including weight, height, and shape. One way to consider body type and size is to consider built environments and ask, "Was this space built for me?" As Roxane Gay notes in *Hunger*, most chairs are not built for her body size, creating significant challenges at work, on planes, and in public settings.
Tribal or Indigenous Status	Tribal or indigenous status refers to whether you are affiliated with and belong to a Native tribe or Indigenous group.

The key to this exercise is to simply notice how much mental space you dedicate each day to these identities and reflect on why. You may notice gaps in the process. I know I did.

When I first completed a version of this exercise in Sukari Pinnock Fitts's classroom at Georgetown's Diversity Management Certification program, I realized that I am in the dominant group when it comes to education (a bachelor's degree and various forms of postgraduate study), and I *never* think about it. When I reflected deeply on it I realized I had created certain barriers and challenges for those in my organization who had not attended college. In talking with them, they felt a distinct lack of belonging based on their education status within the team. One team member described a "secret language" they couldn't access that was rooted in the advanced study both my colleague and I had pursued. Once this realization came to light we could as a team design both individual and company-wide solutions. This included introducing a "gatekeeper" role in meetings who, in addition to making sure everyone had a turn to share, could also call us out when we used jargon or referenced material not everyone had accessed.

REDESIGNING BELONGING

Over the course of 2019 and 2020, the researchers at Sharehold sought out to reexamine belonging, specifically asking the question: "How does uncertainty impact one's sense of belonging at work?"

This question was shaped by the dramatic shift in those years, marked by the global COVID-19 pandemic, the economic consequences of the public health crisis, and the national and global responses to the killings of dozens of members of the Black community.

In the study led by Sarah Judd Welch, the research team surfaced four key findings, including:

1. Uncertainty magnifies the existing experiences of belonging at work.
2. Magnified experiences articulate four types of belonging: Foundational, Self, Group, Societal.
3. Belonging at work is inextricable from power.
4. Belonging at work cannot thrive without healthy workplaces.

The third finding is especially important for our understanding of DEIB. Employers always have power over employees, but in a world where employees have no other safety net to fall back onto, employers have a disproportionate impact on their lives. Employees are dependent on employers who often belong to the dominant group, introducing implicit bias and white supremacy into the same conversations around job security and belonging.

To access the full insights in the report, visit: www.sharehold.co /redesigningbelonging.

MEASURING FOR BELONGING

The first step to building a radically equitable organization that fosters belonging is to measure and understand how the people who power the organization experience it. To see where your organization stands, engage in an assessment and road-mapping process that involves these five core components.

- *Diversity, Equity, Inclusion, and Belonging Survey.* This is a forty-question blend of free answer and multiple-choice questions that measures equity, including commitment, readiness, and self-identification of social identities. The survey allows us to dig into how people experience their organizations by their social identity types, while also aggregating responses to get a picture of the "average" experience.
- *Ethnographic Field Study.* In live environments, researchers from the Ethos team sit in a physical office and observe over the span of one to two days, including shadowing meetings, touring the space, and watching lunch and snack interactions. In remote environments, this involves shadowing video meetings, especially those for blended audiences, and observing conversations in general and open chat channels.
- *Research Interviews.* Formal, anonymous, pre-scheduled thirty-minute interviews with folks leading DEIB efforts within the organization, as well as members of the leadership team. We follow a script to minimize inconsistent data and transcribe faithfully what is shared with us.
- *Office Hours.* Similar to research interviews in that they are anonymous; we follow a script and we transcribe the responses. What differentiates them is we choose one to two days to have essentially an "open door" where

anyone can come and share their experiences with us. This allows us to meet with anyone in the organization, leading to a great diversity of responses in our data set.

- *Cultural Artifact Analysis.* We craft a requisition list of every cultural artifact that relates to set policy, procedure, practice, and structure around an employee's experience at the organization. From there we audit every single piece of material to determine where the organization stands. Generally, we audit anywhere from 100 to 1,000 pages of material.

While we believe that all of this research is necessary when building a long-term strategic roadmap for change, as you begin your own journey to measure belonging in your organization, you can start with a survey, which will be a useful jumping off point.

SURVEY BEST PRACTICES

Many of our organizations have experienced frustration and backlash from their employees when a survey has been released without clear intentions and desired outcomes attached. To make sure you get the most out of your survey, consider the following practices.

- *Create a project brief and team.* Before you send out the survey, decide who will work with you on designing the questions; communicating with all employees before, during, and after the survey; analyzing and synthesizing the responses; and creating a plan to act on results. Generally a project team of two to five people will be both nimble and able to keep responses confidential.
- *Have a plan for repeating the survey over time.* Decide how often you will send this survey out and make sure to include this in all of your communications plans.

- *Socialize the survey with the organization before it goes out.* Before you send out a survey, email the organization and present at an All-Hands meeting, preferably with the support of company leaders. Make sure you have answers to questions around who will see what, where information will be stored, whether the survey is optional or mandatory (we recommend optional), what will happen with the results, and when employees will be able to engage with the findings. Bonus points for explaining how the findings will inform a larger plan, and when that can be expected.
- *Time-box the survey.* Clearly communicate parameters and deadlines. Let people know you are working toward building a plan for change in the next two months, and the only way that will be possible is if we get responses in over the next five business days. And then, remind people to respond two or three times during that period.
- *Offer an opt-in for folks who want to talk about what they shared.* If you want to get at the heart of what is happening in your organization, we strongly suggest to make the survey anonymous. At the top of each of our surveys, offer an "opt-in" where folks can add in their email addresses if they want to talk about what they shared. We make sure to schedule interviews with them after we collect the full results to supplement what we learn.
- *Share the results of your survey alongside next steps.* You have to share the results of the survey with employees. If you don't, they will at best think you were unintentional and reactive in putting it out, which means change isn't coming. At worst, they will believe you are hiding something. Negative reactions are mostly mitigated if results are presented with a plan for a better future.

To support your survey efforts, here is a template version similar to the one Ethos deploys within our organizations to measure belonging: https://www.surveymonkey.com/r/ethosdeib. Customize, modify, and edit the questions based on the needs of your organization.

UNDERSTANDING AND MEASURING
YOUR ORGANIZATION'S INCLUSIVENESS

There is no such thing as a single-issue struggle
because we do not live single-issue lives.
—AUDRE LORDE

────────── PRINCIPLE #2 ──────────

Managers and leaders are now expected to be experts and
advocates on diversity, equity, inclusion, and belonging.

O n May 25, 2020 George Floyd was killed by Minneapolis police officer Derek Chauvin. The grief and trauma of yet another murder in an ongoing onslaught of violence against
the Black community set off nationwide protests. We had seen
similar protests across the country, but this particular instance
had a different impact on workplace conversations. Leaders, managers, and whole organizations were being held accountable by
their employees and their customers in much more pronounced
ways. Simply pledging support was no longer enough.

I remember walking home from protesting in Chicago on May
30th and wondering if it would make sense to give my team members time off to engage in civic action, heal and recover, or just
take a rest from yet another major event to process in 2020. I also

wanted to make sure our existing clients had the tools, guidance, and resources they needed to offer support to their Black employees. I never imagined that by June 1st I would begin the process of talking to forty-one companies in six days.

I had never seen such a big reaction from organizations across all industries and at different stages of growth. At Ethos, we had been quietly navigating the challenges of COVID-19. Our existing clients remained committed to DEIB action, and some were in the process of specifically working toward racial equity, but new clients were hard to come by. The most common argument I heard was: "We have to make enough money to keep employees *employed*. COVID is killing our margins. We'll worry about DEIB later." Plus, in the three years I had been leading Ethos, antiracism was a taboo subject. Any time I suggested starting racial equity work or bringing in facilitators to caucus groups and engage employees in forum discussions around race the response was surprise, hesitation, and sometimes even offense. Part of this, of course, was tied to the fact that the majority of our clients are in the technology space, an industry that is theoretically progressive but practically conservative.[1]

I wasn't alone as a DEIB practitioner experiencing this wave. The top ten bestselling books on Amazon were around antiracism, with Robin DiAngelo's *White Fragility* and Ibram X. Kendi's *How to Be an Antiracist* serving as the subjects of news stories, book clubs, and national discussions. A fellow practitioner, Michelle Kim of Awaken, went so far as to post on LinkedIn a list of the change in inbound traffic to the Awaken website, and a call for all Black DEIB practitioners looking for new clients to share their information so she could pass the requests on to them.

What was happening? Why were companies, almost at the drop of a pin, completely changing their strategies and lining up to make investments?

The answer clicked for me in a conversation with a fast-growing tech company in the compliance space. Pressure from their investors had motivated them to conduct a 40 percent reduction in their workforce earlier in the week so that they could conserve on costs through the end of the year. I was confused about why they were calling, given that a big signal that we won't be engaging with a company is a layoff. One of the organization's leaders put it in stark terms for me: "If we don't make a commitment to anti-racism now, we're going to lose the employees we have left."

He wasn't wrong. Employees, despite tremendous economic uncertainty, were holding their organizations accountable by agitating, organizing, and, when ignored, leaving—all in the pursuit of rapid and radical change around racial equity. For the first time in my career I was overseeing the very public resignations of leaders at my client organizations for failing to take action or holding on to the "way things were."

So, what was leading to a reckoning that businesses arguably had not seen before?

THE COURT OF PUBLIC OPINION

One of our client organizations was ushered into change, including two high-profile resignations, as a result of not just their employees, but their entire community calling for radical reform. They weren't alone. By July 1, 2020, a wave of high-level resignations had taken place across sectors.[2] Among the most notable resignations were:

- Reddit cofounder Alexis Ohanian, who voluntarily resigned in an announcement pledging his role to the organization's first Black board member, Michael Seibel.
- CrossFit CEO Greg Glassman, after outcry around his statement that he was not mourning the death of George Floyd.
- The Wing cofounder Audrey Gelman, amid internal and external pressure.

- *Poetry* Chief Editor Don Share, after the community called for consequences in his publishing of a problematic poem that othered Black and Asian/Pacific Islanders.[3]
- Second City CEO and co-owner Andrew Alexander, in response to alumnus and actor DeWayne Perkins's recounting of racism within the organization.
- *New York Times* Opinion Editor James Bennet, following public backlash over the publication of US Senator Tom Cotton's (R-Ark.) op-ed on the Black Lives Matter movement.
- Adidas's head of global human resources Karen Parkin, in response to Black employees citing a lack of diversity.

THE CALL TO CHANGE

My collaborator and cofacilitator Francine Bailey often brings up a point when we lead antiracism training together: "Alida says George Floyd was different, but I disagree. There are hundreds, if not thousands, of George Floyds. And protests have been happening for decades."

Francine is right. As of November 18, 2020, 986 people had been killed by police in the US, with 28 percent identifying as Black despite the fact that only 13 percent of Americans are Black.[4] In fact, Black people are three times more likely to be killed by an officer than their White counterparts, and the rate of violence is roughly at the same levels it has been for the last five years.[5] As a country, we have also seen widespread protests for many years, as well as a call to value Black lives. Black Lives Matter was officially founded on July 13, 2013, when Alicia Garza, Patrisse Cullors, and Opal Tometi launched the movement-building project in response to the acquittal of George Zimmerman, who had killed Trayvon Martin.[6] Widespread protests in Ferguson, Missouri, resulted after the killing of Michael Brown by police officer Darren Wilson in August of 2014.

This example speaks exactly to the divide in understanding along racial lines in the US. As a White person, I pay attention to the impact of George Floyd's murder on me and people like me. Americans of color have been protesting, marching, and calling for change this entire time. However, a larger group of White Americans are paying closer attention than they have been in several decades. Since White Americans hold more power, the issues are discussed, foregrounded, and addressed differently in the mainstream.

INTERSECTING ISSUES

In 2020, the convergence of a global pandemic, economic downturn, an increasingly volatile political situation, and widespread visibility of police brutality gave rise to a meme popular on Twitter that helps explain why these protests and calls for racial equity finally started breaking through to workplaces. That meme was the "cool zone" (see Figure 4), which refers to a period of political, economic, and social upheaval that leads to the possibility of

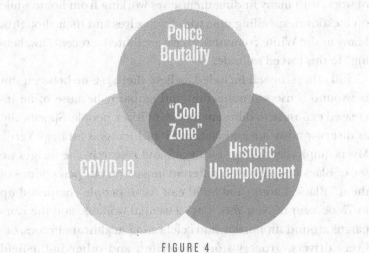

FIGURE 4

emancipation and freedom, especially for those most marginalized.[7] The cool zone's closest analogues in recent history include fighting the Nazis in Hitler's Germany and standing against Jim Crow in Selma.

The intersecting issues that brought racial equity to the fore for non-BIPOC begin with our public health crisis: COVID-19 laid bare major systemic failures in public health that have ravaged BIPOC communities while surfacing larger social determinants of health that are limited in underserved communities, like access to healthcare, food, and education. Around the time of George Floyd's murder, nationally, African American deaths from COVID-19 were nearly two times greater than would be expected based on their share of the population. In forty-two states and Washington, DC, Hispanics/Latinx people made up a disproportionate share of confirmed cases. White deaths from COVID-19, on the other hand, were lower than their share of the population in thirty-seven states.[8] Yet this was a phenomenon that *everyone* was experiencing, which created a shared understanding, sense of grief, and connection among those who previously would not relate to one another. COVID-19 also changed the shape and face of work, with many finding themselves working from home while on lockdown, spending time with themselves and their thoughts. Many in the White community have attributed a recent "awakening" to this forced solitude.

Still others, myself included, believe there is a tie between this newfound sense of connection and empathy because of an increased exposure to different images of Black people. Specifically, as diversity advocate and Netflix VP of Inclusion Strategy Vernā Myers emphasizes in her own work and research, the images we see of Black people have a different impact on our perceptions of them.[9] Black, Latinx, and Southeast Asian people comprised up to 75 percent of New York City's essential workers, and the campaigns around supporting and celebrating healthcare heroes, delivery drivers, grocery store associates, and other in-the-field workers telegraphed to many the role these people played in sacrificing their health for the benefit of others.[10]

These issues were amplified by a serious economic crisis, one that saw weekly unemployment rates soar to as high as 25 percent. The Paycheck Protection Program, meant to support small businesses in the wake of lockdowns and stringent social distancing requirements, was estimated to leave out 90 percent of Black-owned small businesses.[11] Businesses owned by BIPOC have less liquid cash to survive periods like a long-term shutdown, widening an existing generational wealth gap and further endangering Black livelihoods and lives.

These converging phenomena hit their fever pitch when they overlapped with police brutality. The onslaught of so many murders in the weeks leading up to George Floyd's, including the high-profile deaths of Ahmaud Arbery and Breonna Taylor, sparked widespread outrage.

In a 2016 essay, Isabel Wilkerson noted that "the rate of police killings now surpasses the rate of lynchings during the worst decades of the Jim Crow era. There was a lynching every four days in the early decades of the twentieth century. It's been estimated that an African American is now killed by police every two or three days."[12] At the time she wrote this essay, we were still living in the Obama administration, when the term "postracial" was in vogue, and many White Americans did not look for the violence in front of them. By 2020, though, this kind of data was everywhere, and many more people were confronting it head on for the first time.

In a time of multiple crises and trauma, when employees no longer felt a separation between work and life, they brought their experiences, emotions, opinions, and desires around these issues to their workplaces. And that led to an incredible call for action on racial equity as well as on other issues related to social identity, including xenophobia, mental health, physical ability, gender identity and its intersection with caretaker status, and so many more.

WHAT IS AN INCLUSIVE ORGANIZATION?

Your employees expect your meaningful action in issues related to race, social identity, diversity, equity, inclusion, and belonging. Employees no longer view their working lives as separate from social, political, and personal circumstances; in fact, they see work *in the context* of them. When we started telling employees to bring their full selves to work in the 2000s, they didn't just hear that they should bring their senses of humor and hobbies, but the fabric of their identities. The recent crises only deepened the sense among many that *who they are* and *what they do* have to be linked.

You may be feeling a sense of urgency to get things done as quickly as possible. Take it from me, though: acting too fast is a recipe for failure. First you must understand how ready your organization is for change, what those who hold historically marginalized identities in the organization need, and what resources are at your disposal.

In "The Path from Exclusive Club to Inclusive Organization," Frederick A. Miller and Judith H. Katz highlight the importance of a strategic process that creates inclusion for all social identity groups:

> But moving from a monocultural organization to one that is inclusive of all people requires a strategic process. Too many organizations approach it like turning on a light switch—simply wire in the right number of individuals of different backgrounds, styles, genders, races, abilities, nationalities, and other differences, turn on the power, and declare victory/success.[13]

Becoming an inclusive organization is not as simple as turning on a light switch. You may be inclusive of one social identity and not another. The people leading your company might not *want* to include different social identities. There might not be enough representation in your organization to be inclusive. The list goes on and on. So, in keeping with the theme of this section on readiness, the first step is understanding where you stand.

Miller and Katz developed a durable and elegant model for achieving this understanding. Simply called "The Path," it traces all the developmental stages from exclusion to inclusion. The aim is to develop different strategies depending on the stage the organization is at, whether that be focusing on representation, equitable promotion practices and compensation, or mentorship and education.

In the model, there are six developmental stages, each with a set of defining markers (see Figure 5):

Exclusive Club and Passive Club: In this stage, organizations are either loudly monocultural (exclusive club) or quietly monocultural (passive club), with a focus on "fit" and "status quo." In these organizations, employees who are like the founders are more likely to be successful, people feel enormous pressure to fit in and fear speaking up or out, cliques are common, denial of social identity differences is considered a best practice ("We don't see color"), and it's hard to learn how to succeed because nothing is made explicit. In exclusive clubs there is a spoken pride in the way things are ("We only hire from the top fourteen schools; that's why we're so successful"), whereas in passive clubs, monocultural bias pervades all decision-making, but it's not named or celebrated.

Symbolic Differences: This is the stage where difference is introduced. In exclusive and passive clubs, representation of different social identities is minimal. At symbolic differences, more and more people begin to join from different backgrounds, but not in significant enough numbers to feel like they are part of their own group. This stage is marked by "onlies," people who are the "only one of their kind" on the team. These onlies do the labor of disproving stereotypes, answering questions about themselves and educating others on their social identity, making others feel comfortable around them and their differences, serving on committees and special initiatives meant to improve diversity, and of course, doing the jobs they were hired for better than is expected.

Critical Mass: At critical mass, enough members of a given social identity group are part of the organization that the organization begins to shift. The old ways are being eroded, such that existing members of the previously overrepresented group feel threatened. At the same time, new ways have yet to be established. This phase is marked by a tolerance of differences, but also by confusion and change.

Welcoming and Inclusive Organization: The welcoming stage marks a shift from tolerance of differences to acceptance and celebration of them. At this point, the organization truly values diversity (rather than just saying it values diversity) and there is a distinct shift from monoculturalism to multiculturalism. At these organizations, employees are encouraged to contribute differing viewpoints, trust is a given on blended teams, differences are considered additive, people come into contact with each other frequently and consistently, and everyone has the ability to adapt to different cultural contexts rather than asking others to adapt to them. An Inclusive Organization, which is the final stage in "The Path," shares all of these attributes. It's mainly differentiated by how long your employees have been experiencing these markers and how deeply entrenched they are.

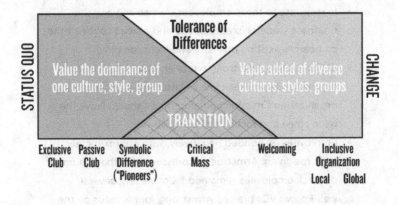

FIGURE 5

A PASSIVE CLUB IN ACTION

If I were reading this book, the first thing I would do is self-diagnose.
So I am going to equip you with an example to help your process.
Let's look at Coinbase's diversity, equity, inclusion, and belonging
story in 2020. Here's a quick summary[14] of what came up:

- Brian Armstrong founded Coinbase in 2012 with a
  mission to advance cryptocurrencies, especially Bitcoin,
  and was involved in designing the organization's hiring
  and training practices from the beginning.
- Fifteen Black employees left Coinbase between 2018 and
  2019 (when the organization numbered around 600
  employees), with at least eleven reporting racism and
  discrimination to HR during their time at the company.
- After the murder of George Floyd in 2020, Armstrong
  did not make a public statement of support for Black
  lives, prompting employees to share their own
  discriminatory experiences at Coinbase, as well as the
  harm they felt as a result of the silence.

- In response to these employees, Armstrong and the Coinbase leadership apologized and agreed to revisit the company's existing diversity and inclusion plan.
- In September, Armstrong wrote an open blog[15] that emphasized that Black Lives Matter was not core to the organization's mission and employees should leave the issue alone and focus on their work.
- Employees responded negatively, with approximately sixty resigning. Armstrong expressed relief that a number of Black employees remained.[16] Conversely, several well-known VCs praised Armstrong for his focus on the organization's mission, especially his emphasis on generating profit.
- Employees reported that the organization had always focused on developing a "consistent culture," where those who thought and acted according to Armstrong's guidelines were prioritized and diversity in the hiring process was not.
- The organization's proportion of Black employees is roughly thirty-one out of 1,000. Of the Black employees remaining at Coinbase, several wrote a report to Armstrong and the leadership team about the state of diversity in the company. No action was taken.

Based on my analysis, Coinbase fits the most defining characteristics of a passive club. Let's go back to Miller and Katz for a moment:

"Passive clubs often pride themselves on 'not seeing differences,' which translates into policies and procedures that reflect their monocultural origins and continuing monocultural bias. Performance management systems, family leave policies, benefit plans and promotion opportunities often favor those who fit in with the founding or leadership group in appearance, style, and behavior."[17]

Since the very beginning of the organization, Brian Armstrong has promoted standards around hiring and training, aiming at consistency over diversity. From a representation standpoint, only 3 percent of the organization is Black, and several Black employees have publicly documented their experiences with discrimination. Armstrong, however, emphasized feeling good about the fact that some Black employees remained. Armstrong's public statement, as backed up by his leadership team, highlighted the importance of not talking about issues of social identity—denying differences—and refocusing on the organization's mission.[18] All of these markers fit squarely into the passive club category.

DIAGNOSING YOUR ORGANIZATION

While the developmental stages in "The Path" are simple to understand in theory, they are much more complex in practice. There are three key principles you must consider when applying "The Path" to your organization.

- *It starts with representation.* I cannot tell you how many people self-diagnose their organizations as inclusive when in reality they have no representation outside of the monoculture. Even if your employees tell you they feel they can bring their full selves to work, are encouraged to share opposing viewpoints, and believe that their differences are considered additive, your organization is not inclusive if you do not have a critical mass of a given social identity group. Critical mass means your employees see enough folks with their social identities in the organization to feel they are part of a group. Without representation you will be at the first three stages rather than the last three.
- *The model is linear; your organization's progression through it is not.* Your organization will move up and down this

spectrum regularly, and your employees will experience different stages depending on their social identities. You may be an inclusive organization for queer employees, a passive club for BIPOC employees, an exclusive club for disabled employees, and a welcoming organization for woman-identified employees. You may be at critical mass, and the backlash from the traditional group forces you right back into exclusive club territory. Conversely, a change in headcount and how those new employees are welcomed and given seats at the table could catapult you to the inclusive organization stage.

- *Diagnose in diverse groups and with outside eyes.* Don't self-diagnose alone: a) bring together a group of people who are different from one another to rate you and b) engage in a spectrum exercise where everyone independently assigns where they think the organization is with three to five reasons why. If this isn't an option, working with a third-party practitioner on this diagnosis is a good route.

If you decide to engage in self-diagnosis, take the third principle to the next level by participating in a short but powerful exercise with teammates:

1. Assemble a group of three to eight people and make sure everyone is versed in Miller and Katz's categories beforehand. Set aside between thirty and sixty minutes for the exercise and discussion.
2. Start by reviewing the key details for each category, from exclusive club to inclusive organization, making sure to leave time for questions.
3. Invite everyone to reflect independently on where the organization falls on the spectrum. Emphasize the importance of taking a holistic view of all social

identities collectively, but note when there are outliers. For example, placing the organization holistically at passive club, but noting that for one social identity group[19] symbolic differences are more fitting and for another exclusive club is a more exact match. Each member of the group should write down three to five reasons why the organization falls where it does in their assessment.

4. If you are physically in the same room, write out all of the stages on separate Post-it notes and present them on a spectrum. Have folks stick up their own Post-it underneath the appropriate stage. If you are virtual, mimic the same experience by using a virtual whiteboard and inviting participants to type where they place the organization underneath the appropriate stage.

5. Spend the remaining time together sharing why each person chose the stage they did, including the three to five reasons they listed independently. Note similarities, differences, gaps, and alternate perspectives. As a group, determine where the organization stands based on the results of your discussion.

BUILDING AN INCLUSIVE ORGANIZATION

The place in which I'll fit will not exist until I make it.
—JAMES BALDWIN

———— PRINCIPLE #3 ————

*Becoming an inclusive organization requires investing
in equity early, consistently, and uncompromisingly.*

O rganizations are not born, they are made. They are often
made in their leader's image. As a career coach, one of the
most common recommendations I make to my clients interviewing for new roles is to remember to ask what the CEO's personality is. This question will often cut through canned responses
around the organization's aspirational culture and help candidates understand the implicit factors that actually shape that culture. As a founder myself, I have seen this play out.

In an early branding exercise with a marketing agency, brand
associates interviewed my employees, family members, and friends
about me. Among the most surprising (at least to me) responses
were "unashamed scholar," "highly engaged," "intense," and
"emotionally generous." As folks joined my team, they found that
these characteristics defined me, and also my expectations for
them and Ethos. I had employees communicate that they felt they
were falling short if they didn't read books and academic articles

outside of work, felt an onslaught of compassion fatigue due to an implicit sense that they should be giving as much emotional support to our clients as possible, and often felt they had to be "all in" on any task they were working on. I didn't *ask* them to do any of these things; they simply felt the pressure that came from working in an organization I had shaped to be inclusive of, well, me.

To a certain extent, this phenomenon is unavoidable until an organization achieves a critical mass of employees. Some residue from the early days always remains, of course, though not in such a blatant and pervasive way. This often results in inclusion stemming from hiring people with the same qualities and values, or at least ones willing to adopt the founder's as their own. This gets in the way of diversity, which in turn impacts potential business outcomes. Accenture's "Inclusion and Diversity Impact" study demonstrates that companies with diverse employee bases see 50 percent greater performance in their teams. Similarly, in McKinsey's 2018 "Delivering through Diversity" report, researchers found that companies in the top quartile for ethnic and cultural diversity on executive teams were 33 percent more likely to have industry-leading profitability, while leadership teams with gender diversity saw 27 percent greater value creation.

The key for businesses at all stages, then, is to involve a broader base of employees to shape the organizational culture, especially so that they can enact their own versions of inclusion.[1] The culture will shift from being directed by one person, often unintentionally, to many who all have stakes in how it operates. This is where equity comes in.

As a quick refresher, equity is a process rather than an outcome. It involves creating the policies, practices, procedures, and structures that allow both equal access and customization based on the very real advantages and disadvantages employees experience on the basis of their social identities. Designing equity practices is decidedly not as "sexy" as launching a new unconscious bias training or publishing a public DEIB statement. They take time and effort that are often underappreciated. They also create meaningful, generational change, including closing wealth, power, and privilege gaps.[2]

ROADBLOCKS TO "THE PATH"

The Miller and Katz model is equity-first. After diagnosis, "The Path" is interested in the strategies and processes that create inclusion and move an organization from one stage to another. In order to make that move, you will face roadblocks that make your journey down the path more complicated. These roadblocks often come from mindbugs, which have to be addressed as you work through the model.

In *Blindspot: Hidden Biases of Good People,* authors Mahzarin Banaji and Anthony Greenwald explain that unconscious bias comes from mindbugs, the ways in which we automatically categorize people based on our own intrinsic brain function. This drive to categorize goes back very far to when we lived in homogenous groups that identified those who looked or sounded the same as safe and those who were different as a threat. We stereotype and judge unknowingly. Yet, mindbugs can be "debugged" if we recognize them, design to overcome them, and root them out.

RECOGNIZE

Deepening our vocabulary when it comes to DEIB issues really does help us recognize our own mindbugs and find ways to be more mindful and inclusive with others.

In *Whistling Vivaldi,* psychologist Claude Steele explains identity contingencies and how they get us into trouble in social groups. While we often see explicit discrimination in companies, more often than not the most pervasive behaviors come from hidden discrimination. Specifically, we associate with and help those who are like us. This tendency comes from identity contingencies, which are the things you have to do within a situation because you have a given social identity. For example, if you are in a group of golfers and you like to golf, identity contingencies are what make you exhibit more "golfer-like" behaviors and associate with other golfers.

Identity contingencies form naturally, even in situations of minimal shared identity, which can make them dangerous because they lead to intergroup bias. In 1971, Henri Tajfel conducted experiments with Michael Billig, R. P. Bundy, and Claude Flament to find out what the minimal conditions were for intergroup bias. They gathered sixty-four male subjects between the ages of fourteen and fifteen and gave them a test to determine how many dots were in front of them. After the test the subjects were grouped into underestimators and overestimators, and then later asked to assign money to two other boys from a shared pot. Because of intergroup bias, the boys gave more money to the boy who had the same designation they had (either underestimator or overestimator), even if it meant all three boys got less money overall.[3]

Another way to think of this is in terms of common affiliations. My husband is a devoted FC Barcelona fan. The affiliation brings him community, excitement, and joy. We start getting into questionable territory, though, when he calls out FC Real Madrid fans and starts making value judgments about them because they support the "wrong" team.[4]

The first step in achieving major DEIB outcomes is to recognize our identity contingencies and notice when we start behaving in an "us or them" mindset. When this happens, there are three questions we can ask to diffuse our own heated, mindbug-based reaction:

- Why am I feeling threatened?
- How is this reaction tied to my own sense of identity?
- Am I responding this way to preserve my ego?

The simple act of reflecting on your current state will help you get above your feelings instead of staying inside of them. With this newfound awareness of what is driving your defensiveness or suspicion around others who are not like you, you have choices. If you have time, psychologists recommend taking a twenty-minute break to regain control of your amygdala. If you don't have time, taking six deep breaths will help you lower your blood pressure and regain focus. From there, note where your threat response is coming from and focus on leaning into a conversation with the other person where you are primarily in the role of listening partner.

DESIGN

When we design for DEIB, there are four practices that help us achieve positive outcomes, so long as we bake them into our planning processes.

- *Information Transparency:* One of the biggest DEIB challenges is that, because of identity contingencies, overrepresented groups tend to have more access to information through their social relationships. If we design for as much information transparency around business metrics, growth opportunities, and team dynamics, we can eliminate the likelihood that underrepresented groups are left out of everything from decision-making to promotion discussions.
- *Solidarity:* Understanding who we are designing for is the first step, not the end destination. We have to invite others to participate in the design process. We must invite employees to help us brainstorm DEIB solutions because they are often a) closer to the problems, with a deeper understanding of them, b) more likely to enact behaviors they were involved in designing, and c) likely to surface ideas that would not have emerged otherwise.

- *Exposure:* One of the best ways to achieve positive DEIB outcomes is to expose people across the organization to groups and individuals outside of their normal sphere. This means bringing product and marketing together or creating meaningful collaboration between sales and engineering as much as it means making sure different genders, generations, races, and ethnicities come together.
- *Social Accountability:* We care a lot about what our peers think, and if we tell them we are committing to a DEIB program, we are much more likely to actually follow it. Whenever we design for DEIB, we have to make sure public commitments happen at every level, especially leadership.

ROOT OUT

If the design stage is all about broader actions and processes, the root out phase is about small acts. In "The Culture Code," Daniel Coyle points out that the shared characteristic between all of the healthy cultures he studied was an overemphasis on saying, "Thank you."[5]

At Ethos, when we are working on big changes, we always start small. To root out mindbugs, one of the first things we do is teach our clients how to listen. We go in depth on active listening and deep listening techniques, which allow us to broaden our perspectives and overcome our limiting beliefs.

For every problem you seek to solve, whether it's a lack of diversity on your team or a culture of interruptions in meetings, always ask yourself one question: What is the root cause? Once you have it, find the smallest, simplest action you can take to start making change.

DESIGNING STRATEGIES FOR CHANGE

Once you have launched a diversity, equity, inclusion, and belonging survey in your organization and have worked with a group to diagnose your stage on "The Path," you may realize you need more information to design initiatives. I recommend focusing on research interviews and artifact audits as you supplement your survey data.

RESEARCH INTERVIEWS

Research interviews are an invaluable tool in garnering your organization's orientation toward DEIB. These thirty-minute interviews with folks across the organization lead to richer, more specific insights and often help contextualize survey data, surface inconsistencies in experiences, and allow for the development of new and different ideas. I have proposed some of my most daring and creative initiatives as a direct result of recommendations in these interviews.

For scheduling these, we recommend having both "open hours" where anyone can interview with you or members of your group, as well as pre-scheduled interviews with leaders who will impact outcomes, employees who are driving for change, and at least some folks who are ambivalent, neutral, undecided, or even against DEIB. We like to have at least twelve interviews for our assessments, which allows us to hear from a diversity of people and understand differences in readiness. Some organizations require three or four times as many interviews; others don't. It depends on the size and stage of "The Path" of an organization. As you begin conducting interviews, you will have a sense of how many you need.

At Ethos, we have a standard research interview template we developed in alignment with our own qualitative research training. We regularly customize it once we have context on an organization and a broad understanding of where it sits on "The Path."

It is absolutely critical that folks stay on script and don't editorialize, share information from other interviews, or launch into questions without orienting research subjects first.

RESEARCH INTERVIEW TEMPLATE

Guidelines

Hi, my name is [INSERT NAME], and I lead [INSERT ROLE DESCRIPTION] at [INSERT ORGANIZATION NAME]. My focus today is to conduct research and synthesize information to provide an external view of the organization's current state when it comes to DEIB and make recommendations for opportunities in the future.

The purpose of this interview is to capture information about the organization's culture and DEIB readiness from your perspective. You may have differing views from colleagues, which is natural. We don't expect you to share those views instead of your own.

To record your responses, we have two options. I can, with your permission, record what you share using my Zoom app and then transcribe your responses. I can also record your responses manually by typing the transcript as you share them with me. Which do you prefer?

Your responses will help shape our overall assessment of the company's culture and orientation around diversity, equity, inclusion, and belonging. They will be reviewed and analyzed in conjunction with other interviews, an anonymous company survey, and an artifact audit.

These interviews are anonymous, not confidential. We will not list your name in our materials. However, members of my team will have access to interview transcripts and we may quote parts of your interviews in our assessment, which will be shared with the company. If you wish to share information you want off the record, simply let us know, and we will strike it from our transcripts.

After the interview, you are always welcome to email us with follow up questions, comments, and information.

Questions

1. Tell me about your role at the organization.
2. How would you describe the culture of the organization?
3. How long do people stay here? Why do they stay?
4. When people leave, what reasons do they give?
5. What kind of people succeed here?
6. When things go wrong, what do you do as a company? How do you respond?
7. Do you feel you belong in the organization? Why or why not?
8. Does the organization invest in a sense of belonging? If so, how?
9. What is the organization's current orientation toward diversity, equity, inclusion, and belonging?
10. In one year, what would success in diversity, equity, inclusion, and belonging look like for the organization?
11. What is the current biggest obstacle to enhancing the organization's commitment to DEIB for you? For your team? For the entire organization?
12. How would you rate your readiness to invest in diversity, equity, inclusion, and belonging?
13. How would you rate the Executive Leadership team's readiness to invest in diversity, equity, inclusion, and belonging?
14. How would you rate the majority of employees' readiness to invest in diversity, equity, inclusion, and belonging?
15. Is there something I didn't ask that I should have?
16. Is there something you'd like to ask me?

ARTIFACT AUDITS

While research interviews are tremendously helpful, they are filled with gaps. Often respondents haven't had access to information around policies and procedures, which makes the artifact audit so powerful. At Ethos, audits help us understand what infrastructure we're working with and whether employees understand it.[6] Our audits include:

- *Hiring Processes:* We evaluate how job descriptions, career pages, and candidate messaging are written, noting any words or phrases that send implicit or explicit exclusion signals. We also audit where jobs are posted, how they are advertised (and to whom), and the way the applicant tracking system is configured, including whether it collects Equal Employment Opportunity Commission data. We review what applications ask for, who makes it through each interviewing stage and in what proportion by social identity. We ask what each interview stage looks like, what questions are asked, who is on the hiring team, whether they have been formally trained in interviewing, and what that training contained. We also audit how candidates are scored and rated, how hiring team members engage with one another during the interviewing process, how background and reference checks are conducted, and how negotiations and offers are handled.

- *Compensation:* We look at compensation across an organization, analyzing the data for an understanding of consistency in titling, leveling, base salary, benefits, and other forms of compensation. We audit this information with an eye on social identity and market data.

- *Employee Handbook:* We focus on what benefits exist, who they impact and support, and how they are explained and detailed. We also evaluate what procedures exist to respond to harassment, bullying, or discrimination, looking to see which social identities are explicitly protected. We audit whether the organization's vision, mission, and values are included and how its policies clearly outline expectations for employees in their roles. We look at accountability measures in the employee handbook that hold employees to its policies, including discrimination, and also what holds employers accountable to their employees.

- *Performance Management:* We evaluate what performance management looks like in the organization, including what systems are used, how people are rated and measured, how often they receive feedback and whether it is documented, what direction that feedback goes (top-down, bottom-up, peer), what language is used, whether social identity–based stereotypes appear, and how performance management ties to compensation. We also look to see if there are growth plans or career pathing documentation that charts how employees can improve their performance, get promoted, and receive support in the process. We audit Performance Improvement Plans, including who leads them, how they are distributed (including by social identity type), what guidance is offered to those who have been placed on them, how frequently they are used, how long they last, and how many people complete them in good standing versus being terminated.
- *Exit Interviews:* Some organizations keep documented exit interview transcripts, which we read and review for patterns and themes. We often create a spreadsheet where we code reasons for exit, suggestions for improvement, and calls for action, as well as what worked within the organization.

- *Any Assessment, Survey, or Workplace Polling Data Given to Employees with Results:* Whether it's on culture, the workplace environment, employee engagement, or experience, we look at existing data to understand whether there has been change over time, what key themes and insights emerged, and how consistent responses are with one another and our other research.

While these make up the backbone of any audit we conduct, we often find that to get at the heart of an organization and its commitments not just to its employees but its broader community, we have to get creative with other kinds of audits. These include:

- *Publication History:* About a third of our clients are nonprofits and/or arts and cultural institutions, many of which publish magazines. For one of our more prominent clients, we audited seventeen years of magazine issues to determine representation of editors and guest editors, authors published, and subject matter addressed.
- *Programming:* Depending on the level of access we have, we can sometimes run programming audits where we evaluate what events and programs an organization has led, including who they were designed for, who attended, how they were reviewed by attendees, subject matter, accessibility, where they were hosted and why, and how all of these factors mapped to social identity. For example, one of our organizations counted over half their community as Black grant recipients, and about 65 percent of their learning programs were designed specifically for these individuals and hosted in the neighborhoods where they lived.
- *Customers:* For really ambitious organizations, we have looked at who their customers are, what they do, whom

they represent, who is represented within them, and with what ideologies, industries, and other institutions they are affiliated. For one of our customers, we saw that they represented congresspeople in almost equal proportion (Republican vs. Democrat), which was reported out to the company. For another, we identified two customers funding private prisons, which ran counter to the organization's mission and goals, leading to a reevaluation of those contracts.

- *Board Composition:* We have audited board representation against our twelve social identity types as well as what organizations board members were affiliated with, their involvement in other boards and community organizations, their history of decisions within the organization, and what public statements they have made in the past.

The key with audits is to know what questions you most want to answer. We looked at magazines, for example, because members of the community emphasized in an open letter and in research interviews that the organization owed a debt to Black writers. How could we quantify that debt? One answer was to audit the magazine's writers. Similarly, we found through an exit interview audit at another organization that woman-identified employees left at twice the rate as man-identified employees. The reasons for departure included both lack of role models and access to education. We audited what training programs existed, who was invited to them, and how that impacted their careers.

For organizations and people inside them who don't have previous audit experience, the steps after data collection can be unclear. What do you do with all of this data? What should you be trying to find?

The answer is straightforward and can be broken into three important steps:

1. *Look for trends, patterns, and themes:* Cluster like information with like information, sorting to understand that broad patterns are in the data. Label these patterns as you go. For example, let's say you noticed that four out ten people who recently left your organization—or 40 percent of exits—cited lack of flexibility and long hours. You would label that something like "Work and Life Balance."

2. *Report out your findings:* Once you have conducted your audits, grouped, themed, and named your data, and gathered it together in one place, begin sharing the results with others. You may choose to start with members of a DEIB Committee or a leadership team. In that report, seek out their perspectives, responses, and questions, which can help you dig into additional data and start collecting actions to take. Once you have a sense of how you will take action on the findings, make plans to share them with everyone in the organization in a listening session.

3. *Take action.* With the data and responses from the report-out process mapped, it's time to translate ideas into action. Using the models below, develop strategies for addressing gaps and disparities, as well as seizing opportunities. For example, if your customer audit turned up a number of customers whose goals run counter to DEIB, explore a new vendor agreement and a process for ending contracts. Or, if your programming audit showed an opportunity to feature more BIPOC men on panels and in fireside chats, compile a list of experts and begin reaching out with paid opportunities.

INTRODUCING R2P2

Now, with a more robust set of data, you can start designing what initiatives to invest in. While I encourage you to consider how to impact your community and customers, even at this stage, I always want to share a deeply held belief. An organization that is not equitable internally is more likely to design practices that perpetuate existing power structures. Start first with your immediate community inside of your organization, and then look outward. This minimizes the risk of diversity fatigue and helplessness in the face of having so much to do in the world. For this reason, at Ethos we start with a general assessment of readiness, culture, and existing DEIB practices, and then launch into recruiting, retention, promotion, and protection.

R2P2 is a simple model we can use to make sure we're taking a full picture view of our organization. The reason it works is because it doesn't just break out where we should be looking, but also underscores that we need to be balancing several different parts of the employee experience instead of overindexing on one. R2P2 breaks down into four key areas:

1. *Recruiting* focuses on the people, processes, and resources necessary to identify, attract, and hire to build diverse teams.
2. *Retention* ensures employees stay happy, engaged in their work, and committed to the organization.
3. *Promotion* focuses on the tools, resources, strategies, and compensation decisions that ensure team members can move up the ladder and remain aligned with the organization.
4. *Protection* is focused on the policies, training, resources, and technology necessary to make employees feel safe.

When you use R2P2, keep in mind what's already working in your organization. There's no sense in throwing the good out with the bad, especially when it can teach you to structure improvements in the future.

The exercise we recommend for companies trying to incorporate DEIB into culture is R2P2 Mapping. First, gather the team that has been working with you on the assessment to put together your first version. Afterward, we recommend working with leadership to deliberate on, debate, and decide on R2P2 again.[7] Then, bring the whole organization together in their own workshop to chime in. In each group, you will grid out the four R2P2 pillars. Start by looking at all the positive practices in place in your current state. For each category, think about what's really working, write it down, and discuss *why*.

From there, look at what you could lean into more in the future, where there are gaps, and where you might grow in the future state. Simply capturing all of this information is the first step in building a lightweight, easy-to-follow DEIB plan. The whole process takes no more than an hour for each sit-down.

R2P2 MAPPING

R2P2	CURRENT STATE (WHAT'S WORKING TODAY)	FUTURE STATE (WHAT TO WORK ON IN THE FUTURE)
Recruiting		
Retention		
Promotion		

R2P2	CURRENT STATE (WHAT'S WORKING TODAY)	FUTURE STATE (WHAT TO WORK ON IN THE FUTURE)
Protection		

CREATING A DEIB PLAN FOR THE FUTURE

Once you have mapped out **R2P2**, keep the momentum going by organizing the information into a plan. Simpler is better and the fewer the ongoing initiatives, the more likely they are to actually come into being.

A sample DEIB Action Plan can be found at http://www.alidamirandawolff.com/bookreaders.

PART TWO
IDEAS INTO ACTION

The most challenging part of diversity, equity, inclusion, and belonging is translating ideas into action. Conducting an assessment is vital for understanding root causes, making a diagnosis that surfaces the right actions, and gathering the evidence to support your decisions, especially in the face of resistance. And yet, as much as people ask to see the data, what they *want* is to see marked change in their day-to-day working lives.

After conducting hundreds of research interviews, I have concluded that most folks in organizations know what they need to do, they just don't know how to do it. Their "gut feelings" about lack of representation or barriers to advancement are proven out by the data, and then they are left with the incontrovertible proof of a problem they do not know how to solve.

It seems simple. If you didn't see enough woman-identified candidates for enterprise sales roles, build strategic partnerships with three to five community organizations supporting them, rewrite your job descriptions, post on different job boards and on the social media platforms candidates actually check, and recalibrate your interviewing process to minimize bias.

But that's the theory, not the practice. In practice, there are always three obstacles that make seemingly simple suggestions like these very, very challenging: time, resources, and stakes.

- *Time:* Creating cultures of belonging and launching diversity, equity, and inclusion solutions take time, and if there is one thing no organization I work with has, it's time. Employees maximize their time by doing more work that drives more revenue in tighter and tighter timeframes. Try telling an overworked, time-starved sales team failing to meet their quotas to engage in a three-month-long hiring process that will result in modest gains in the short term. Even if it will pay off seriously in the long term, you are going to meet some resistance.
- *Resources:* Whether an organization is actually underresourced or has the mindset that it is, resource constraints will hamper simple solutions. Most of the solutions you develop will cost something: money, working hours, energy, clout, or opportunity. No matter how conservative the effort, you need a budget to do DEIB work. And most companies don't have a DEIB budget in place, which means to drive initiatives there is a certain amount of navigating ambiguity, competing with other teams and initiatives for backing, and deciding whether to engage in uncompensated work outside of normal hours.
- *Stakes:* The stakes are different for almost everyone involved in this kind of change. Those who are happy with the way things are (and there are many people who fit this category) will not prioritize the work or provide meaningful support (low stakes). Those who are most negatively impacted by the way things are may object, scrutinize, and challenge because they are thinking of

their own lived experience, or they may have given up because of exhaustion, transforming them into single-issue voters who derail change (high stakes). Then there are all of those people who find this to be important, but don't feel comfortable with or understand the roles they must play (mid stakes). This group of allies can be mobilized, but identifying who they are and what will mobilize them is a process. Then, there is the element of hierarchy in all of this. If the organization's decision-makers count themselves as part of that low-stakes category, no matter how straightforward the solution, getting there will be hard. On the flip side, if a few leaders are driving *everything*, very little will change because employees have to be brought in and be active too.

I am not sharing any of these obstacles to dissuade you. I genuinely believe that security blooms when people have all the information at the beginning and can anticipate challenges, struggles, and roadblocks early.

I also believe in belief. If belonging matters to you (and I know that it does) the strength of your belief can be harnessed and leveraged to do unimaginable things.

In the next few chapters, we are going to go on a journey together through culture-building, recruiting, retention, promotion, and protection. I am going to break down exactly what frameworks to use, what actions you might (or might not) take, and what opportunities and roadblocks you may encounter along the way. Some of it will feel easy and other parts will feel hard. What matters is this: I know that you can do this.

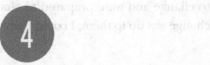

PREPARING FOR CHANGE

Alone, we are food for the wolves.
—FRENCH PROVERB

———————— PRINCIPLE #4 ————————
If you introduce change into a system
too quickly, the system will reject that change.

W hen I started my diversity management program at George-town's School of Continuing Studies, I never expected systems thinking to be my biggest takeaway. It was a mode of thinking I was familiar with from work in organizational health and transformation; and it was embraced by technology teams I knew and understood. But it had never been taught to me formally, and when I finally had the chance to sit with it and process the systems I was part of, a missing puzzle piece fell into place.

For years, when I heard other DEIB practitioners and change agents in organizations tell me a client wasn't ready for change, I took them at face value. I didn't apply this mindset to my own clients, though. Everyone was ready if I tried hard enough—the key word being "I."

But when I came to understand systems thinking, I realized that no one "I" could change a system, especially one outside the system.

I could guide, direct, and advise, but only organizations that wanted to change and were prepared to change, would. The decision to change was up to them; I could help with the preparation.

LEVELS OF A SYSTEM

The first step in translating ideas into action is preparing for change itself. To prepare for change, you have to understand two things: there are many systems at play, and within each system are levels. A system has set boundaries, its own structure and purpose, an overarching ideology, and a way of doing things. An organization's culture is a system.

Within any given human system are groups of people. People within groups are drawn together by a sense of shared identity and the cumulative and mutual experience of having that identity. Marketers share an identity tied to being the kinds of workers who attract and retain customers through a variety of different but related strategies. They may relate to one another based on how they are perceived by others for being marketers and actual experiences they had as marketers, like putting together a campaign or struggling to report out marketing attribution. The same logic applies to social identity groups. Latinx people share an identity tied to their cultural heritage, and they may relate based on their cumulative experiences of being perceived as Latinx by others, whether that might be assumptions around their first language, likely professions, or family ties.

LEVEL	Individual	Group	System
EFFECT	Bias	Discrimination	Ism
WHO IS AFFECTED	Individuals in 1:1 relationships	Everyone within a particular or set of particular social identity groups	Everyone inside the system

Within social identity groups are individuals. Individuals define themselves in terms of their self-knowledge and also what they know of others. Experience at this level is much more one-to-one than at the group level. For example, a conversation about pay equity between a woman-identified individual contributor and a man-identified manager takes on a different flavor if it's happening at the individual versus group or system levels. At the individual level, the conversation is about how they relate to each other. The woman may point out that she is due for a raise, and the manager responds that he needs to see improvement in her communication skills. In turn, she could say that this feedback is ambiguous or that she disagrees and feels unfairly passed over or even that she will work on those skills between now and the next review cycle. At the group level, however, the conversation takes on a different character. In response to her manager denying the raise, the woman could point out that the gender pay gap means that women make only 81 cents to the dollar their man-identified counterparts do, and being underpaid is part of her lived experience as a woman.[1] At the system level, this conversation may be part of a much larger set of policies, practices, and structures rooted in an organizational culture of male supremacy, which may also contribute to shorter leave times, opaque compensation standards, and an unstated policy on how to manage negotiations.

Belonging and levels of a system go hand in hand. I can feel that I belong with my group and in my group, and that because of my group identity, I cannot achieve a sense of belonging within the system. If I want to achieve that belonging, I may have to reject my group identity. As Mia Birdsong puts it, "More of us are permitted entry to the club if we do the double duty of conforming to its standards and continuing to meet the ones set for us— women must lean in, queer couples must get married, people of color must be master code-switchers."[2]

At the individual level, we experience bias. Everyone is capable of bias; it's human nature.[3] As a White person, I have experienced bias from BIPOC people. One of my toughest resistors was a Black man who said that he could not take my work seriously because as a White person in DEIB I was the equivalent of an "overweight personal trainer" or "R. Kelly with a relationship counseling business."[4] He expressed a bias against me because I am White, even though being White puts me in a position of power and privilege.

What I can't experience as a White person, though, is discrimination and racism. At the group level, we see discrimination on the basis of group identity. Discrimination is "the unfair or prejudicial treatment of people and groups based on characteristics such as race, gender, age or sexual orientation."[5] What's important here is that the group has to be marginalized in order to be in this position because the rules are not made by them or for them. They are part of a system where members of the dominant group can use the tool of discrimination to keep existing power structures in place. The marginalized group simply does not have enough power to discriminate on a grand scale, though they can engage in acts of bias that create barriers, limitations, and challenges for members of the dominant group.

At the system level, we see isms like racism, sexism, ableism, heterosexism, and so many others come into play. An ism is different from bias or discrimination because it is not isolated to an act or a series of acts. Rather, it's a pervasive way of thinking and doing things. Racism is an invisible hand that ensures BIPOC have less power than White people, and it shows up in decidedly impersonal ways that impact the greatest possible number of people. Discrimination, as stated, is a tool of racism, which we can see in everything from housing and healthcare to employment and policing. But racism itself is not calling someone a slur or denying them entrance to a business.[6] While it creates the conditions for both circumstances, it is ultimately "the cumulative and compounding effects of an array of societal factors including the history, culture, ideology, and interactions of institutions and policies that systematically privilege white people and disadvantage people of color."[7]

Here's why these levels of a system matter so much for translating ideas into action.

When you are designing actions, you must understand what level you are working within.

If you don't, the action could be a drop in a bucket that doesn't create much change at all. Yes, positively impacting one employee from a marginalized group is huge, and scaling belonging means positively impacting as many of these employees as possible. Scale requires system-level change that is informed by group experience and individual voices.

When you are talking to someone from the individual level and they are speaking from a group level experience, you will miss each other.

How will you create change if you are talking past each other? I have made this mistake over and over again. In a workshop I was leading on overcoming bias and engaging in upstander intervention, I presented data from a study that showed men interrupted women significantly more than the other way around. One of my man-identified participants physically turned his chair away from me and crossed his arms while telling the person across from him that he did not believe my data. I asked him why (but only after defending my data set longer than I should have), and he said, "Because I had four sisters growing up, and they all interrupted me. I don't interrupt women ever." I was talking at the group level, while he was talking at the individual level. What I should have done differently is pointed out that when I asked who related to this study, the four woman-identified participants raised their hands, with one saying her experience as a working woman was to be interrupted by men on a regular basis. These women weren't talking about *him*, but their cumulative experience of their shared identity.

> When you understand the levels of a system, you know who, how, and what to prepare for change.

Individuals will have different experiences, motivations, and interests than their respective groups when it comes to belonging. Some groups may be ahead of others, and they are very likely to be ahead of the system in terms of being ready to embrace change. A People Operations leader can work with their CEO at the individual level to get the necessary buy-in to build structural changes that support one or more social identity groups because of the system-level impact. Their actions will be different for each one. They may have to work with their CEO on mitigating resistance stemming from lack of information, caucus different social identity groups to understand how they experience the structures and policies that govern them, and then develop the organization's policies and set up accountability practices that ensure they are enforced.

OVERCOMING RESISTANCE

Resistance is real, and if you learn to confront it head-on early, you are so much more likely to create a culture of belonging across your organization. We need each other to move together, and while we may not be able to get every last person on board, we should be trying for collective buy-in and action as much as possible.

To paraphrase the incredible adrienne maree brown, none of us are special, and all of us are needed. No one "I" is going to create belonging for all, but one "I" *can* mitigate and manage resistance to allow the group to enact change. This is perhaps the most important role a change agent can play and, in my experience, it's also the least understood.

What is resistance? Like power, it's just energy in a system. It isn't good or bad. Resistance can lead to freed and collective emancipation. Resistance can also be a setback, roadblock, or challenge to positive change. What matters is what is the resistance to and where is it coming from.

In *Beyond the Wall of Resistance*, Rick Maurer lays out the three levels of resistance and support. At level one, support looks like folks understanding what we're talking about. At level two they like it. And at level three they are confident and trusting in us. For our resistors, the opposite is true. They communicate their resistance as "I don't get it" (level one), "I don't like it" (level two), and "I don't like you" (level three). To transform resistors into supporters, we have to identify what type of resistance they are showing us, and then engage in actions to help sway them into support.

Years of experience have taught me what resistance sounds like. There are a few phrases that trigger my spidey sense. This is by no means a comprehensive list, but it can be a useful key, especially when navigating multiple points of resistance taking on different forms throughout the process.

WHAT THEY SAY	WHAT THEY MEAN	TYPE OF RESISTANCE
"We don't have enough information to make this decision."	I haven't thought of this before, and I don't know what's happening.	
"What is the scope of this issue?"	What's going on? Is this a problem?	
"Do we really have a problem?"	As far as I know, things are going well here.	I don't get it.
"Won't this resolve itself organically?"	This is a minor issue that can be resolved on the individual level.	
"I don't think this applies to us."	I am not seeing evidence of this issue in my day-to-day.	

WHAT THEY SAY	WHAT THEY MEAN	TYPE OF RESISTANCE
"It's a shame so many other organizations struggle with this, but that doesn't mean we do."	I accept this is a problem for others, but I don't think it is for us.	I don't get it.
"If you share these results, won't that make people needlessly worry?"	This information opens up a conversation I don't want to have.	
"I don't think we are ready for this."	I am not ready for this.	
"What's wrong with being proud of our culture? Why can't we celebrate who we are?"	I like the way things are, and I don't want them to change.	I don't like it.
"We don't have the time for this."	This isn't a priority for me or the organization.	
"We are already doing good work on this."	Don't invalidate our efforts or suggest we don't care.	
"What makes you the authority on this issue?"	You aren't qualified to lead this and don't know as much as you think.	
"My point of view hasn't been factored in."	You don't have my best interests at heart.	
"Why aren't we hearing from other people about this?"	You have your own agenda you're trying to advance.	I don't like you.
"Give someone else the floor."	You are monopolizing the issue, which makes you untrustworthy.	
"What do you have to gain from this?"	You only care about your own personal gain.	
"Maybe we should get an expert opinion."	I don't trust your judgment.	

Identifying the type of resistance is not always straightforward. Sometimes you're met with resistance at multiple levels, or folks act like they are resistant for one reason, when internally they are resistant for another. I believe that at least half of my outwardly "I don't get it" resistors are actually "I don't like it" resistors. This is because in modern organizations, it is more socially acceptable to say, "We don't have the data to make this call" than "I like us just the way we are."

Similarly, you might guide someone through level-one resistance, get them on board, and then watch them descend into "I don't like it" territory when they realize what they will have to give up to make change possible (time, energy, resources, power). You might trigger their defenses at some point, escalating resistance into the "I don't like you" zone.

The key is to ask questions and really listen. Start by gauging their understanding of what is happening and what is being proposed. Have they actually seen and reviewed all the data? Have they been engaging in learning activities? Did they show comprehension then and now? Is this a big or small roadblock they are putting up? All of these questions will help determine if you're in level one, two, or three. From there, you can trace whether they are responding to your proposal or to you.

Once we understand the type of resistance, we can choose our best tool for overcoming it. Level-one resistance requires facts, data, more information, and learning. The reason training and development programs can be so effective is that, in most companies, resistance comes from ignorance. Once employees achieve greater awareness, they are much more likely to get behind initiatives. Level-two resistance requires empathy, which means taking the time to gauge where they are coming from, listen to them and show resonance, validate them without agreeing, and, ultimately, make them feel so understood they are willing to understand you. For me, level three resistance is the hardest because it can involve personal, mean-spirited attacks and because humans are hardwired to fear social rejection. To go up to someone who you know dislikes you and be vulnerable and authentic takes a lot of confidence and coping skills. Even at this stage in the game, I struggle with it.

TYPE OF RESISTANCE	WHAT IT MEANS	HOW TO OVERCOME[8]
I don't get it.	The individual doesn't fundamentally understand what is being said/described/ taught	Logic
I don't like it.	Arguments are rejected based on internal feelings about the subject matter	Empathy
I don't like you.	Your thoughts, ideas, examples are rejected based on your personal impact on the other person	Authenticity

LOGIC

Level-one resistance is the easiest to overcome; it requires the kind of solution we are most used to having at work. We are constantly asked to present the data, rely on the facts, collect the information, and explain ourselves. We have the muscle memory for a logic-based solution.

The best way to use logic is to understand where the gaps are. I am a stickler for information, and I am regularly asked to pull back and share *less* data because I am overwhelming others. True story: when someone challenged a recommendation I made and asked for the data behind it, I produced 1,081 pages of evidence. This came off as a power move,[9] and, it took them a lot longer to process than if I had drilled in and asked: "What's missing for you here? What would you need to see to better understand?"

Learning style matters in this approach too. Some people need to process information independently and in a written form. Others are visual or auditory learners who need the information presented in different formats, including in groups where they can hear what others have to say. Still others need to think out loud and brainstorm in order to fully gather what's happening. I find that folks often need stages of information—context on the issue, data on how it impacts their environment, and stories (preferably from others they know) to cement the information as real. To get the most out of a logic-based solution, ask about learning styles to design a share-out that guides people through what they need to know at a pace and level that works for them.[10]

EMPATHY

In her essay "Lonely in America" for *The Fire This Time*, Jesmyn Ward's anthology about race, Wendy S. Walters writes:

> Paying attention often requires some sort of empathy for the subject, or at the very least, for the speaker. But empathy, these days, is hard to come by. Maybe this is because everyone is having such a hard time being understood themselves.[11]

There is a reason that at Ethos, behind "Upstander Intervention" and "Developing Racial Competence," our most popular training is "Empathy" followed by "Leading with Empathy." Everyone wants to be on the receiving end of empathy, even if they struggle to show it for others.

In managing resistance, empathy is an invaluable tool because it helps earn trust. We want people to listen closely enough to be changed by what they hear, but we need to be willing to reciprocate. This reciprocity, as a reminder, is an inherent tenant of belonging.

As Mia Birdsong points out in *How We Show Up*, empathy involves learning to make space for people. That means changing the language we use. For example, instead of defaulting to "Let's look on the bright side," or "Are you sure that's what's happening?" shift to phrases that show solidarity: "I'm sorry that happened to you," or "That sounds hard." Listening without judgment and with a willingness to let the person on the other side of the conversation express themselves without having to defend, debate, or persuade is a gift. And gift-giving is an inherently reciprocal way of engaging with others.

For a long time, I said my single greatest accomplishment in DEIB was a "conversion" of an entrenched resistor. This was a leader who was absolutely resolute in not giving alternative perspectives a chance in the realm of social identity and equity. Then, in a public forum, his own CEO called him an anti-Black racist who supported the police because of its history of violence within the Black community. These were meant to be fighting words, but instead of provoking the spirited debate the CEO was hoping for, they sent his second-in-command directly out the door. I followed him, and what proceeded was a two-hour conversation where he expressed his anger, sadness, and conflictedness as someone coming from a White working-class family that dug its way out of poverty through careers in the force. In this conversation, he shared views like, "I don't believe in race; I believe our society is postracial"; "We all have the same twenty-four hours. It's what you make of them. It's as simple as that"; and "I voted for President Trump, and I am being treated like a criminal for it." I did not agree with his views, given my previous work with detention centers and the incarcerated, but I also knew this was not the time to argue with him. I engaged in something I call "validating without agreeing," where I affirmed his feelings as real and probed more deeply into them. Three-quarters of the way through, I noticed a shift. He said, "Thank you for listening," and then he asked me about my experiences. I decided to tell him about my own scary experiences with power and violence. I noticed how open he was to hear me mention topics he previously would not entertain. Two months later I watched him in a group of all White men tell them he was successful because he was White, man-identified, cisgender, and young and healthy, and that he knew his life would be very different if he wasn't born with that "invisible knapsack of privilege." He then proceeded to teach them a social identity exercise I lead in most of my classrooms, including one he sat in. Surprised, I asked him what prompted this change. He actually said, "You listened to me, so I thought it was important I listened to you, too. And, I changed my mind about some things. Then, I started listening to other people, and that changed my mind about a lot of things."

There are a few things to call out in this example. I chose empathy for someone in the dominant group. I made this choice because I believed I could get through to him, had a relationship with him that mattered to me, and understood that getting over this hill with him would lead to widespread positive impact in his organization because of the amount of influence and power he held.

You might not feel moved to do this, and I don't blame you. If you are coming from a marginalized group, you may feel you are asked to adapt to the needs of those in dominant groups so often, to explain your oppression to those who oppress you, and to simply do work that shouldn't fall to you. In these situations you have choices. Kevin L. Nadal has outlined a three-step process for determining what to do when you are personally impacted by microaggressions that applies more broadly to any identity-related situations:[12]

- *Step One: Did this resistance really occur?* Sometimes, it's obvious that you are experiencing resistance. Other times the situation is more ambiguous or nuanced. For example, if a woman hears someone whistle as she walks down a street, she may think, "Did that really just happen or am I hearing things?" When there are people around whom you trust, ask them how they would label the situation. When there is no one around, seek support from your support system, sharing the details with folks over the phone, text, email, or social media to get a wider variety of opinions.
- *Step Two: Should I respond?* If you are certain that resistance is happening (as I was in the previous examples), consider the risks you may face in engaging. Some questions to ask yourself are:

    If I respond, could my physical safety be in danger?

    If I respond, will the person become insurmountably defensive?

If I respond, how will this affect my relationship with this person? Does this relationship matter to me?

If I respond, will it feel emotionally or psychologically exhausting?

If I don't respond, will I regret not saying something?

If I don't respond, does that convey that I accept the behavior or statement?

If I don't respond, will this person impact me and the people around me negatively?

- *Step Three: How should I respond?* If you decide taking action is the right path for you, consider the approaches available.

  Deflection: Use humor to diffuse the situation and point out the resistance's impact on others nonthreateningly. This is a good strategy if your energy is limited but you want to say something.

  Direct Intervention: Call out the behavior or resistance without worrying about what Nadal calls "calmly addressing" the person. If you feel frustrated or angry and releasing your true feelings is therapeutic, that's an option too. Just remember to first reflect on the questions in step two.

  Assertion: Tell the person how they made you feel and describe why their behavior is impacting you. This may result in defensiveness that leads to offensive or harmful behavior, so decide how much you want to engage and when to leave the situation. Using "I" statements and avoiding value judgments ("You're a racist! You're a sexist! You're a bigot!") in favor of pointing to specific behaviors can help you meet in the middle. It's important that while this is happening you think of your support system and mentally note that you will process and seek care from them after the conversation reaches its end.

AUTHENTICITY

The hardest part about an authenticity strategy is that when folks are either explicitly or privately against you, putting yourself out there feels unnatural. Why would you open yourself up to someone who is already rejecting you? This is where we need to go back to trust. If they can't know what the future of DEIB and belonging in their organization looks like, they have to understand your motives and intentions, believe you will not act against them or others who matter to them, and trust that you care. The power of vulnerability is that when you let down your defenses and show your cards, others are more likely to do the same.

There are two effective ways to be professionally authentic when confronted with resistance, and they should go hand-in-hand. The first is to transparently and clearly name why you do what you do and what your personal stakes are. The second is to make promises and keep them. Both require time, energy, and effort.

In one of my facilitated sessions with an affinity group I was supporting in developing strategic initiatives, a member paused the session to call me out. I was waiting for this moment because she had been the main resistor to initiatives and actions in the group, putting up blocks to any idea associated remotely with me. She started by explaining that she was frustrated and offended by the direction I was taking the group, and then she said, "I don't know; it's like . . . I don't think you have any integrity." I took a breath, and then I responded like this:

"Thank you for bringing this up in the group because if you feel this way, I am sure others do, too. I want to start by apologizing. I can hear that I have not made you feel seen in my approach, and that my attempts at outreach outside of this group were not enough. I also want to acknowledge that when I steered us away from your recommendation, I made a mistake. I am sorry. I really care about this organization; I think that means I can overidentify and become a participant rather than a facilitator. I see so much potential for belonging here. I promise to spend more time facilitating turn-taking and consensus. I will invite this group to adjust our meeting norms to hold me accountable."

I followed up by working on updated meeting norms, sitting on my hands when I felt like making a suggestion without asking the group first, and continuing to lead with why what I did mattered. She and I mended our relationship and collaborated on a plan that is still alive in their organization.

DIALOGUE AND RESONANCE[13]

To prepare a system for change, the members of that system have to learn a new way of communicating with one another. The first change that should take place is around language and listening. That's why the dialogue and resonance framework is so essential to any vision around scaling belonging.

Developed by Debra Alexander, Suzanne Anderson, and Kaye Craft, and influenced by work on relational culture by Cedar Landsman and Lucién Demaris, dialogue and resonance is a technique designed to support connection, conversation, and thoughtful action. Through disciplined and concerted dialogue, participants practice communicating without the goals of winning, persuading, or deliberating. Instead, they concentrate on generating the greatest amount of ideas and information, making space for various perspectives, engaging in deep listening, and thinking as a collective. In dialogue, participants are expecting to have their minds changed, no matter what roles they play.

Resonance is what makes all this possible. As Alexander, Anderson, and Craft point out, "resonance is a relationship skill, and a process that helps to shift culture." Resonance involves taking

time during deep listening to notice when you feel most connected with what you hear. Once you have noticed that connection point, you express it through "I" statements. Some of these
statements include:

- "I felt really connected with you when you said . . ."
- "What really impacted me was . . ."
- "What most resonates with me . . ."
- "I felt right there with you when . . ."
- "I heard you and felt . . ."
- "I related to you when . . ."
- "What most struck me was . . ."

In the spaces I lead, I use dialogue and resonance to focus
only on generating ideas, reaching nuanced understandings, and
expressing connection. This means operating with a few well-
telegraphed guidelines that are messaged before and during our
time together:

- We don't make meaning or interpret; instead, we take
  what we hear at face value.
- We can ask broad, nonleading questions for the
  purposes of clarification. We do not ask leading or
  challenging questions.
- We do not shift attention to ourselves until the floor is
  given to us and it is our turn.
- We answer share-outs with resonance rather than our
  own stories or experiences. We know there will be space
  for our stories and experiences later on.
- We reserve opinions, judgments, and comparisons.
- We offer support, understanding, and care, not advice.
- We watch for and avoid comparative grief, competition,
  or any divisive language that separates "we" into "you"
  versus "me."

Of every activity I have led in small groups, this is the one people take away and try on their own because the information they get is richer and the sense of connection stronger. This technique reads simple on paper but can feel wooden and weird in practice. You have to try it out multiple times to get it right.

I recommend introducing this activity as an opener to any meeting where decisions are being made, just to help folks build the muscle for it so you can use it for larger and longer sessions.

Activity: Dialogue and Resonance

Time: Twenty minutes

Number of Participants: Three per group

To set this activity up, assemble in groups of three. You will have a speaker, a resonator, and a timekeeper.

Each person speaks for three minutes about a question. They must speak without interruption, even if that means rambling or making things up as they go.

Suggestion Question: What feelings are invoked in you when you hear the word "belonging"?

Hold the three-minute timeframe even if the person finishes before the time is up. Often after several seconds of silence, the speaker may wish to add something further.

As the first listener speaks, they begin with a statement of resonance to the previous person before beginning what they want to say.

The listening partner has two total minutes to respond.

Once the first cycle is complete, rotate roles. You will cycle through until every person has played every part.

CREATING A CULTURE OF BELONGING

Systemic oppression relies on the careful partitioning
of social space. Specifically, it requires that
marginalized peoples . . . dwell within corners, that
we shrink inside walls that loom and compress.

—RACHEL VORONA COTE

PRINCIPLE #5

Too often, our vision, values, and mission exist solely on our walls
and our company websites. What matters is that we define them with
our employees, and then develop behaviors we can all live by and
share in daily, weekly, monthly, quarterly, and annually.

As much as starting with an easy, quick win in DEIB is valuable,
the greatest rewards come when organizations look closely at
their vision, values, and mission (VVM) and ask how it may
need to transform to help shape change.

An organization's VVM is how it sets targets and aligns to its
highest purpose. If done correctly it also defines, steers, and ce-
ments culture. Since culture determines who experiences belonging and disseminates the practices necessary to live out diversity,
equity, and inclusion, scaling belonging begins with a community-
driven process of reevaluating or cocreating its VVM.

One of my favorite questions to ask employees when I kick off an engagement at a company is, "What is your vision statement?" I always get a slew of totally different answers, at least half of which are some expanded version of the company tagline. This is true at the leadership levels too. I can't tell you how many CEOs don't know their vision or haven't even actually defined one.

What never fails to surprise me about a VVM is how polarizing it seems to be. I spend my working hours talking about diversity, equity, inclusion, and belonging, mediating conflict, leading major change management initiatives, and coaching people through the most stressful moments of their careers. Yet nothing gets people more upset than reflecting abstractly on their VVM.

I think the reason this small set of words inspires such strong opinions is because of the fact that so much has to be said with so little, and the stakes are very high in getting it right. When done well, a VVM achieves clarity, direction, and alignment for a company—three things that take on outsized importance as that company grows, when it's harder and harder to be high-touch with each employee. A sense of shared purpose is the foundation of a commitment culture, which we know is the most successful organizational model for risk prevention and growth opportunity. A VVM can give us that purpose by clearly stating why we do what we do, how we want to get there through our approach and behaviors, and what that looks like practically in terms of what we deliver. When employees get to be part of the experience of answering all three of these questions, the impact is even greater because understanding shoots through the roof along with a sense of ownership.

The challenge with VVMs is we don't end up crafting them truthfully, authentically, or specifically enough for those words to mean much to anyone who wasn't part of writing them. Consequently, they can end up looking like office dressing. Even if people actually understand the words, there's always the question of what we do with them. Healthy culture is all about actions. We have to leap from drafting the VVM to coming up with the behaviors that will make it come true in real life.

Please take a moment to write out your company's why, how, and what in as few words as possible, and then designate clearly actionable behaviors everyone must take part in to make them true.

Of course, that means getting that why, how, and what right and making sure everyone in the company knows what they are and can get behind them. Achieving that level of clarity is absolutely key to determining that you and your teams are a match.

WHY BUILDING A CULTURE OF BELONGING MATTERS

At the height of the tech bubble from 1994 to 2001, James Baron and Michael Hannan analyzed the founding cultures of 167 tech companies through the Stanford Project for Emerging Companies (SPEC).[1] Together, they identified five organizational models these startups put in place on their paths to IPO.

The most common model was the professional model, where folks specialized in a particular skill (in this case, engineering), followed by the star model, which prioritized hiring the best and brightest employees. Further down the list was the commitment model, which emphasized informal peer-group control, shared values and emotional bonds, and focusing the hiring process on culture. Only 7 percent of all of the companies invested in a commitment model.

However, despite its unpopularity in startups, the commitment model turned out to be the winner in terms of companies successfully heading to IPO and surviving tough economic conditions. During the course of the study, the tech bubble burst, shutting down many of the companies studied as part of SPEC. However, at the end of the study, none of the commitment-model companies had closed, while the failure rate for the rest landed at 13 percent.

> Not only that, but the companies most likely to have an IPO were commitment-model companies.
>
> Companies where employees care about and live the culture are not just the ones that survive; they're the ones that reach the greatest heights.

WHAT VISION, VALUES, AND MISSION MEAN TO EMPLOYEES

When I worked in my venture firm, I gave my team my heart, soul, and health. I believed deeply in our vision of creating a people-first approach to investing that was focused on helping entrepreneurs grow and scale their businesses. From day one, I knew that's what we were working together to do. It helped me weather our own startup-like storms: long work weeks, huge priority shifts, role ambiguity, and exhaustion-induced conflicts.

In my last year there, I felt something happening to my commitment level. I still believed in the vision, but I no longer understood my place in achieving it. It wasn't until we finally brought in an external coach to lead our own workshop on our vision, values, and mission that I realized what was happening. We were defining our values together, and our coach had written our top choices on the whiteboard. We had just finished force-ranking them when she looked at me and said, "Alida, I can sense you're unhappy with these. What's up here that's causing your reaction?" There was nothing we had chosen I didn't believe in. My problem wasn't what was written on the board, but what *wasn't*. Humility. Kindness. Thoughtfulness. The three things, I realized in that moment, mattered most to me.

Our vision originally attracted me to the role and motivated me to give it all I had, which fundamentally benefited the organization. But my personal values didn't match up with our company values. There wasn't anything wrong with either of our ways of being or the behaviors we believed were necessary for a healthy organization. It's just that we could have gotten to a better outcome if we had known about this mismatch sooner.

INTENTIONAL CULTURE IN PRACTICE

For many of our clients, "intentional culture" is an oxymoron. Culture is supposed to be organic, natural, and self-evolving. This was true of an events-based agency that, after eight years, had become one of the fastest growing companies in the US.

For much of its life, this company had hovered at about thirty employees. It was the kind of place where everyone gathered together each day for "Family Meal" and connected casually and constantly over everything and anything in the business. They organically came together and collaborated well, which led to resistance in formalizing structures or ways of working together.

The way the leadership team saw it, a vision wasn't necessary because anyone could talk to the founders at any time about what they were trying to do. Hiring was slow and everyone had a chance to participate. Performance feedback didn't seem important when everyone had access to continuous feedback from peers, leaders, and their direct reports. Unknowingly, an organization that didn't believe in architecting culture had architected a good one through regular ongoing practices.

Then, the company went from thirty to 300 in two years. This explosion validated the company's business model, more than proved product-market fit, and served as a magnet for people who wanted to be part of a "rocket ship" on its way to making major moves. And for the first time, people problems started to crop up and create roadblocks. Turnover increased, client experience challenges emerged, and workplace conflict and silos developed full force. Employees reported feeling excluded, underappreciated, and for the first time in what was an exceptionally diverse organization, like DEIB didn't matter.

The company was built to scale, but the culture wasn't.

With 300 people, six physical offices, and founders who needed to be with each person and at each office at the same time, sitting around a communal table to hash out ideas over a lovingly prepared meal just wasn't an option. Who could even coordinate all of those schedules?

But this was a team that started their own company because they hated corporate culture. The mention of "HR" didn't just give them pause; it made them question the point of their own growth. They wanted to be part of a fast-moving, energetic, creative, bold environment, and they didn't think any of those words applied to the cultures they'd seen at the big companies they had been part of in the past. Yet they understood something needed to change.

A major reason those other cultural models wouldn't have worked was *time*. With the pace of change in this company, rigid systems just wouldn't have been adopted. Employees didn't have the bandwidth to put them in place or maintain them. We also didn't have the resources from team members we needed to create anything complicated to support culture. Instead, we figured out exactly what a company like this one needed to create a healthy environment where employees would thrive.

In four months we created lightweight guideposts for their culture. We began by defining what a good shared way of life would be, and then we involved all 300 employees in shaping the vision, values, and mission, along with all of the regular practices we could put into place to make the words we crafted come true in real life. We broadcast these practices across the company and made sure they were tied to tangible actions and outcomes.

We also collaborated with motivated team members from across departments and business lines to run an Appreciation Taskforce, which focused on making employees at all levels feel appreciated. Finally, we developed three systems designed to lower

employee turnover, increase engagement, and alleviate interde-
partment tension. We created a more inclusive interviewing process that involved more than just the founders in hiring decisions
and emphasized project interviews, created an onboarding process
any manager could lead that would make sure new hires didn't feel
like they had to "sink or swim," and built a performance feedback
process that didn't require too much tech or financial investment.

By the end of the four months, they had a People and Culture
department, employees who felt more included and appreciated,
and the mental space to seize on company growth opportunities.

STARTING WITH WHY

There are many models out there for crafting a Vision, Values,
and Mission, but the simplest and easiest to use isn't even one
originally created for that purpose. In Simon Sinek's *Start with
Why*, he explains that too often we start with *what* when we should
start with *why*.

This ordering comes down to practicality. If our brain is broken
down into two parts, our limbic brain and our neocortex, we need
to pay attention to what each does when it comes to information.
Our limbic system, which is the oldest part of the brain, is where
most emotions live. It's also our decision-making center. When
someone says, "trust your gut," they're actually saying, "listen to
your limbic brain." The neocortex, on the other hand, processes
information and is responsible for language.

Your limbic brain tells you what to do, while your neocortex
justifies that decision with language.

Another way to think about this comes from Michael Gerber in
The E-Myth: "The truth is, nobody's interested in the commodity.
People buy feelings." If you're trying to sell something, whether
it's an iPhone or the company's new direction, you focus on what

people want to *feel*, not a feature set. You want your employees to work for you because they believe in what you believe, not just because they need a job. You want to build a shared culture, inside and out, that's on the path toward change you've set.

If we use Simon Sinek's model, we can think in terms of our "why," "how," and "what" (see Figure 6):

- Why: Your why is based in a purpose, cause, or belief. Why does your organization exist? Why does that matter to others? This idea of mattering is crucial here because it's what sets off that "Hell Yes!" or "Hell No!" in others to help them determine if they're in this experience with you.
- How: Your how is made up of special qualities and characteristics that set you apart. How do you do things differently? How do your values, guiding principles, and beliefs help you achieve your why?
- What: Finally, your what is literally what you do—the products or services you sell.

Your vision, values, and mission are the more presentable, communicable outputs of your "why," "how," and "what."

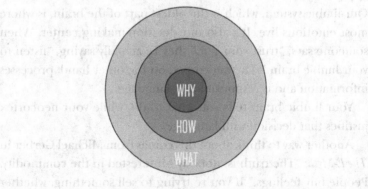

FIGURE 6

Your *vision* is what would happen if your "why" were to come to life. What do you aspire to be as a company? The key to a really good vision is that it's never complete. Your mission can end, but your vision is what drives you forward. Pick something big and broad enough to take you far into the future.

Your *values* are those actionable characteristics and behaviors of "how" you will achieve your vision. They are the way you want to do what you do.

Your *mission* is the current state of "what" you are doing to bring your vision and values to life. This is the part of the circle that changes the most. Perhaps you go from being a one-cause nonprofit to one with many causes, or a consulting firm that becomes software-as-a-service. The output is different, but it's likely that the vision and values are closer to the original versions.

Taken together, the vision, values, and mission form your company's purpose statement, which guides every decision you make in your company.

As your company changes, pivots, transforms, and grows, you will need to revisit your VVM at least annually, acknowledging that other than your mission, you might go long stretches of time before you adjust your vision and values. Maybe they will always hold true. Or maybe they will change several times because you're figuring the organization out. The key is to revisit these and check that they are setting the appropriate direction for the company.

A Purpose Statement template can be found at: http://www.alidamirandawolff.com/bookreaders.

EXAMPLE VISIONS AND MISSIONS

Vision Statements

Ikea: To create a better everyday life for many people.

Life Is Good: To spread the power of optimism.

Nike: Bring inspiration and innovation to every athlete* in the world. (*If you have a body, you are an athlete.)

ServiceNow: We make the world of work, work better for people.

Tesla: To accelerate the world's transition to sustainable energy.

Mission Statements

Patagonia: Build the best product, cause no unnecessary harm, use business to inspire, and implement solutions to the environmental crisis.

ReelGood: To be the place that people go to when they want to watch any TV show or movie.

Sweetgreen: To inspire healthier communities by connecting people to real food.

LIVING YOUR VISION, VALUES, AND MISSION

Once you've crafted your purpose statement, you're ready for the most important phase of the visioning process: developing behaviors to live by with your company. Remember, a VVM means nothing if it can't be put into practice.

While you may choose to leave your employees out of the purpose statement development process, it's essential you include them in setting key behaviors, preferably in an interactive, company-wide workshop. This will establish a greater sense of connection to the company, fellow employees, and the overall behaviors. The latter is especially important because employees need to buy in to the values in order to actually live them.

COMING UP WITH BEHAVIORS

Typically, to designate company behaviors, you will want to focus everyone's attention on values. It's best to have three to five values so that employees can actually remember them.

Since deadlines and cadence help establish expectations, scope, and accountability, we always advise our clients to assign daily, weekly, monthly, quarterly, annual, and ongoing tags to each behavior they choose. We also recommend between ten and fifteen behaviors per value, with the most successful companies (in terms of adoption) landing at five to seven behaviors per value. The behaviors you choose should be a combination of ones that are currently already happening and ones you aspire to incorporate into your organization. It can be useful to break these down into "Current State" and "Future State" if you are really angling for change. Leaving them combined has its own advantages, especially if you're hiring; new hires assume everyone is engaging in these behaviors and adopt them right away:

- *Daily behaviors* are ones that would be easy to perform each day and would be additive. For example, if your value is "Teamwork Makes the Dream Work," a daily behavior might be "We will deliver continuous feedback in short bursts," or, "We will say thank you to our teammates."
- *Weekly behaviors* are usually tied to structured activities that already have a cadence or work best with one attached. If your value is "Quality," then you might choose a behavior like, "We will address areas for improvement in our weekly Standup," or, "We will review customer feedback as a company on Mondays."
- *Monthly behaviors* may require more work to complete or are tied to cross-collaborative initiatives. For our company that chose "Work Harder, Play Harder," one of their behaviors

was to celebrate everyone's birthdays once a month because it was easier to have one big celebration than several small ones. Another company chose "Team" as a value and committed to putting together department metrics each month that everyone in the company could review.

- *Quarterly behaviors* can be tied to board activities, revenue reviews, and strategic planning. At Ethos, our "Always Learn" value is tied to a commitment from all of us to teach each other a new concept or skill at the company offsite.
- *Annual behaviors* are where holiday parties, summer bashes, and team-bonding activities fall, though like with the other examples, it can encompass more. For one of our clients who chose "Have Fun" as a core value, the behavior that ended up in this category was the Summer Olympics, where each employee could compete in silly, accessible, office-inspired games one Friday each year.
- *Ongoing behaviors* don't fit neatly into a time box but are critical to creating the kind of culture that will allow the company and individuals to flourish. Some of my favorites that came out of a customer-centric value are, "We always say yes to customer requests if they make sense," and, "We share customer emails across the team."

LEADING A VISION, VALUES, AND MISSION WORKSHOP

There is no workshop I love leading more than a company-wide Vision, Values, and Mission, because it's where I get to hear employees tell their favorite company stories, fight for what matters to them, invest in the company's direction, and ask questions they've been sitting on and now finally have the opportunity to pose. No matter which company I lead these workshops in, I see employees leave more committed than when they walked in.

It's better to hire an outside facilitator for a company-wide workshop because it means everyone has a chance to participate in the experience together. Still, companies do lead these workshops internally and can do a great job of it, especially if they keep the structure simple.

Any good VVM workshop should be broken up in three parts:

1. *Context:* The designated facilitator, ideally an employee who is perceived as neutral, has the ability to hold a room's attention, and is skilled at mediating, introduces the Start with Why model and reviews either the proposed or existing VVM. They take questions and suggestions.

2. *Brainstorm:* The facilitator breaks employees up into teams and asks them to start by identifying current behaviors that support the company's values. In bigger settings, the facilitator asks each group to focus on one value instead of all of them. Once employees have had enough time to discuss and label these current behaviors, they switch over to thinking about future behaviors and follow the same steps.

3. *Group Share:* Each group presents what they came up with and takes questions and suggestions from the audience. Group members make modifications in real-time, and the internal facilitator takes notes on everything else others share.

At the end of the session, the facilitator lets everyone know that they will put all the findings from the workshop into an editable document each employee can see and publicly comment on for one week. After that period, the facilitator will make final changes and updates, and share the finished product with the company. From there, the company will decide how to implement newly introduced behaviors and elevate existing behaviors in a public forum, like a Townhall Meeting or through a general chat platform.

THE POWER OF PERSONALIZATION

Nothing grips an audience more than personalization and customization. When audience members feel like you see them and understand their interests, they really tune in. We see this in our VVM workshops all the time, which is why in the planning stage we always ask three key questions:

1. How do people on the team learn (for example, through research and fact-finding, visually, through reading, or by doing)?
2. What is one thing everyone in the room has in common besides that they work for the same company (for example, Harry Potter fandom, a love of outdoor activities, or a common company mascot)?
3. What is some company-specific language or slang employees use all the time (for example, calling each other crew members instead of teammates)?

We have gone to great lengths to personalize these workshops for companies, using Shark Week, Burning Man, and even pineapples—yes, the fruit—to make them feel tailored to our audiences.

By far, one of the most successful company-wide VVM workshops we led was for a software company that had sixty employees all obsessed with *Star Wars*. When we talked about why culture matters relative to risk, we used the Galactic Senate as our case study, emphasizing that Senate members didn't enforce rules or values transparently and consistently engaged in a culture of back-room dealing, leading to eventual corruption and the takeover by the evil Emperor Palpatine. After that example, we didn't see a single iPhone screen or laptop open for the rest of the two hours.

CREATING A CULTURE CODE

Once we craft our Vision, Values, and Mission together, we take them a step further and put together our own Culture Code. This is essential to achieving the alignment we need to move quickly. It also lays the foundation for better hiring and for a smoother experience when we inevitably have to part ways with some of our employees.

In a nutshell, a Culture Code is a living document that employees contribute to over time that builds on a VVM to establish the norms for treating each other within an organization.

The basic structure of a Culture Code is:

- *Purpose:* What is the Culture Code meant to do at your company?
- *Structure:* How is the Culture Code structured to achieve its purpose?
- *Vision:* What is your company's vision for the future?
- *Values:* What are your company values, along with the behaviors that represent them?
- *Mission:* What does your company do?
- *Principles:* In addition to your values, what standards do you live by as a company? For example, if "Build a Better Future" is a value, what set of principles might employees follow to achieve that value?
- *Practices:* Which behaviors have you assigned to each value? How often are people expected to engage in these behaviors?

- *Expectations:* What do you expect employees to do, and what can they expect you to do as their company? In other words, what are the unspoken rules that govern your culture? Are you a headphones culture where no one can tap you if you have headphones in? Are newcomers expected to come into their first week prepared to debate or sit back and listen?
- *Contributions:* How can everyone contribute to culture in different ways?

Once you've captured all of this information in a public, centralized repository, whether it be an internal wiki or a shared document, let people know they can leave comments, suggestions, and questions at any time. Make it a practice for leadership to review the Culture Code on a quarterly basis so they can respond to any comments or questions that come up, with periodic spot checks to make sure key issues are addressed as they come up.

When you make a Culture Code accessible and open, it signals to everyone on the team that they are part of developing the culture and their voices will be heard, which inspires more commitment, ownership, and participation.

RECRUITING

We are our choices.

—JEAN-PAUL SARTRE

---------- PRINCIPLE #6 ----------

*A DEIB recruiting strategy creates the space for
a diverse, equitable, and inclusive workforce.*

T he recruiting process is long, arduous, and energy-consuming.
As much as my clients say they "love" hiring, they rarely mean
it. They love meeting new people. They love being asked to
be part of making decisions. But when they're deep into interviewing, they are often overwhelmed, confused, and distracted. I
don't blame them. Most people get thirty to sixty minutes to decide if a person they have never met before is the "right" person
for a job that they may not fully interact with, relate to, or understand. They also tend to rush. They're hiring because they need
someone to do a specific set of tasks *now*, and the work of hiring
is often more than they'd planned so they are likely to fall behind
in their own day-to-day responsibilities. This sense of urgency, of
course, is a recipe for bias.

The combination of urgency, uncertainty, and personal stakes
makes the prospect of referrals in the hiring process very appealing. Forty percent of hires are made based on referrals, with up to

85 percent of new hires reporting that they acquired their roles through networking.[1] We are more likely to trust the people we know. We are also more likely to know people like us, which means "the best person for the job" is often coming from one or more dominant groups and shares a lot in common with the person who referred them.

I am not exempt from this. We have a rule at Ethos: the hiring team must name their biases before we meet with candidates, so the group can hold them accountable. This rule was largely developed because of me and my own sense of self-awareness.[2] I tend to favor Latinx, woman-identified young people with similar skill sets and aspirations to mine, and I am always subconsciously imagining my mentees when considering new hires. We still allow referrals to come in, but they can't "skip the line"; they still have to go through the same application process, that application has to be reviewed by someone on the team who does not know either them or the person who referred them, and if all of us know them, we *all* have to review the application and come to consensus.

You may notice that there are an awful lot of interventions taking place before interviewing even happens. That's because hiring is critically important; your employees are your cultural cofounders, the difference between successful business outcomes and unsuccessful ones, and the core of your organization. Hiring impacts not only your organization, but also the people you hire.

I remember being in a debate with a fellow DEIB practitioner about the importance of hiring in structured equity work. Her belief was to hire as many BIPOC employees as your organization would allow, no matter how exclusive it was; mine was that if the organization was toxic, exclusive, and racist, the system needed to be repaired and restructured before introducing unsuspecting new BIPOC employees to harm. I was convinced I was right until I started digging into the crux of her argument that physiological needs come before safety, love and belonging, esteem, and self-actualization. Even though families of color will soon make up a majority of the US population, the racial and ethnic wealth gap is staggering. Specifically, White family wealth was seven times higher than Black family wealth and five times higher than Hispanic family wealth in 2016. That's a bigger gap than in 1963.[3] In other words, worry about making your organization more inclusive to marginalized groups, warn prospective candidates about the current state of the organization, and answer questions about issues of social identity openly and honestly. But don't preemptively "protect" or factor out marginalized groups. That kind of thinking may further widen the gap and hurt candidates from these groups generationally rather than just in the short-term of a recent job search.

HOW TO BUILD AN EQUITABLE AND INCLUSIVE HIRING PROCESS

Since hiring is so important for everyone involved, it begs the question: How do I do this well? What does a responsible, equitable, and inclusive hiring process look like? It starts with understanding that you can have anything you want, but you can't have everything. You can attract a broader range of people, provide a thoughtful and caring experience to them, and see the impacts on a more diverse and engaged pool. But you can't ask for it to happen in two weeks' time. This kind of hiring is not and will never be fast. It will, however, get *faster* once you land on your process, use it a few times, make sure everyone is trained on it, and refine it to work out any kinks and gaps.

To help accelerate this process, here are the stages of what I consider to be an inclusive and equitable hiring process:

1. Design the Role
2. Assemble a Hiring Team
3. Develop the Interview Stages and Scorecard

4. Create a Hiring Communications Plan
5. Write and Publish Job Description
6. Evaluate Applications
7. Interview Candidates
8. Conduct Reference Checks
9. Make an Offer
10. Onboard the Candidate

The following stage breakdowns feature, to varying degrees, how to ensure this process foregrounds social identity representation and equity. As you move through them, though, remember they are meant to be considered in conjunction with these questions:

- What would make this stage explicitly antiracist? Antisexist? Anti-ableist? Anti-ageist? Anti-elitist? Anti-xenophobic? Antiheterosexist? Anticlassist?[4]
- Who belongs with me at this stage? Who ought to make decisions with me?[5]
- Where are my biases and gaps? Where are the team's? The organization's?
- Are my must-haves actually nice-to-haves? What is truly essential for this role versus what prioritizes people who are like people who already work here?
- How are we using language to open or close doors to marginalized identities? What are new and different ways to use language?
- If every person involved in this process could see how I am running it, would I be proud of what they saw? Would they find shortcuts or cheats? Where?

DESIGN THE ROLE

Before automatically reposting the same job description used to hire the person who is leaving or copying a standard description from peer organizations, take a step back and understand what the team really needs. Break out board decks and the annual strategic plan, review the business model and your team's target metrics, and think about what capabilities currently exist and do not exist on your team. Then start answering these questions:

- What are this role's core objectives? How are they expected to achieve them?
- What kind of targets will they be expected to hit, and how quickly?
- What will they inherit (a book of business, a dysfunctional team, a marquee customer, or legacy software)?
- Which of the responsibilities will be temporary versus permanent?
- What will you be able to teach this new person? And, what realistically, will they need to know without your help or training?
- What resources will be available to them? What resources won't they have?
- What is the makeup of the team they are joining? How experienced or skilled is this team?
- What is the team's culture like? Who succeeds in this culture? Who doesn't?

Once you have the answers written down, you will have the skeleton of a new role description. To flesh out that skeleton, start by diving into each objective. What is it? Why is it important? How does it need to be achieved? With these answers in tow, gather more information about the role. Talk to team members in similar positions, allow other team members with expertise or applicable experience to weigh in, and reach out to peers who have hired to meet similar objectives at other organizations.

CULTURE FIT VERSUS CULTURE ADD

The speed at which language falls in and out of favor causes my clients major whiplash. One VP of People described it to me this way: "I used to get yelled at unless I talked about the importance of culture fit in interviews. Now, when I say the words 'culture fit,' people look at me like I've just said a bad word. What happened?"

What happened is that language is appropriated, reappropriated, adapted, and shifted over time, evolving its meanings.

"Culture fit" has come to be associated with conformity, assimilation, and fitting a round peg into a round hole. It's also often poorly defined in organizations, which allows for bias to infiltrate cultural conversations. Now, the term "culture add" has replaced it.

Culture add is associated with diversity because it focuses on developing a process where the organization's principles are codified and documented; how people are evaluated culturally is based on procedures, standards, and competencies rather than "gut feeling"; and difference is embraced rather than dismissed. *Culture fit* is about whether you are like the people here; culture add is about whether you believe in the same principles the organization upholds.

We can tie this distinction back the broader discussions of culture in chapters one and five. A culture of belonging is one where anyone, regardless of social identity type, can experience opportunity to access and mutual respect. They may choose not to take advantage of this reciprocal relationship, but that is a choice they get to make, not one the organization makes for them. What matters is that they are *aligned* with the vision, values, and mission of the organization, and that they are contributing value. That's at the heart of the culture fit and culture add switch. The first South Asian man to join a company may not "fit in" to the culture, but he may add so much.

ASSEMBLE A HIRING TEAM

Depending on the size, stage, and cultural environment of your organization, assembling your hiring team is either the easiest or hardest part of the process. The hiring team is made up of the folks who will collectively run the interviewing process. Keeping these teams small, focused, and close to the work candidates will do is essential.

ROLE	NUMBER	DESCRIPTION
Hiring Manager	1	The Hiring Manager is who the candidate will report to once hired. This person designs the role in the first stage and leads the interview and evaluation stages, even though others will be involved. They may also screen applications and conduct reference checks depending on how much support is available for recruiting.
Recruiter (Candidate Advocate)	1	The Recruiter (or what we like to call "Candidate Advocate") is the person who communicates with candidates throughout the process, and they may review applications, conduct phone screens, manage reference checks, and coordinate team schedules for interviews.
Peer	2-3	Peers are folks who would work directly in this role. They conduct behavioral interviews to exchange information about the role, the organization, working styles, and expectations. They also participate in final interviews when appropriate, and their ratings are considered at an equal weight alongside the Hiring Manager's to make a final decision.
Optional: Direct Report	2-3	For roles that will manage others, involving direct reports is critical. These folks will conduct the same kinds of interviews as they would in a peer context.

I am often asked how diverse the hiring team should be. While I think there is value to the candidate experience of introducing folks from the same social identity categories into interviews, proceed with caution.

Every candidate should, to the extent possible, interview with the same hiring team members so that the comparison is apples to apples. Don't bring in extra woman-identified interviewers for woman-identified candidates; factor social identity into the hiring team makeup from the beginning. Also, don't misrepresent diversity in your organization. If the team this person will work with is not diverse, they should know that going into the organization. In fact, the team members interviewing them should let them know, too, and how they plan to address it. Finally, be mindful of who you are asking to do the work, and whether you are tokenizing them. Underrepresented employees often get asked to do more work outside of their job responsibilities (like recruiting) than their overrepresented counterparts, which works against them because they are more likely to be overworked, underpaid for their contributions, and overlooked for advancement since so much of these "extra duties" don't get factored into their performance evaluations.

DEVELOP THE INTERVIEW STAGES AND SCORECARD

Once the hiring team is in place, decide on how many interviews you plan to conduct, what the aim of each will be, and how you will measure candidate performance along the way. While I like to customize interview questions and project types for different roles and teams, I typically stick to the same structure of interviews.

- *Applications:* I ask between three and five probing questions about the skills needed for the role, the candidate's values, and the opportunities they see for the future of my organization. I develop the application questions and requirements well in advance so I can accurately estimate the timeline for a given role.
- *Initial Screen:* This is a thirty- to forty-five-minute interview where the Recruiter or the Hiring Manager asks a blend of questions that determine whether the candidate has the baseline skills to meet the job

requirements and investigate who they are, what they value, and how interested they are in the role.

- *Technical Interview:* We prefer our technical interviews to follow a generalizable format and avoid test-taking mechanisms, especially since marginalized groups are more likely to experience test anxiety and have experience with discriminatory tests. In this forty-five-minute interview the Hiring Manager asks the candidate to present a project they are particularly proud of. Candidates are notified that they will be asked to present this at least forty-eight hours in advance. The project must be something they have actually completed, and it should also be relevant to the job requirements. After the first twenty minutes presenting, the interviewer will dive in with deeper questions about the project, as well as deeper career experience.

- *Behavioral Interviews:* We interchangeably call these interviews "Peer Interviews" and "Culture Interviews" because while they are designed to leverage behavior-based questions, they are conducted by the prospective candidate's would-be peers, and help the interviewee understand the organization's culture. These are typically thirty minutes long. In advance, the Peer Interviewers should get on the same page about what questions each will ask. This will help corroborate what is shared and develop a deeper level understanding of the candidate.

- *Project/Case Study Interview:*[6] This sixty- to ninety-minute interview led by the Hiring Manager and Peer Interviewers aims at allowing the hiring team to understand if the candidate has the hard skills to do the day-to-day work of the role and how they collaborate with the team. The candidate will receive a case scenario based on an actual problem the team has tackled before (such as designing a new program, fixing a website bug, or handling a challenging customer complaint). They will be asked to solve for certain goals, bring a presentation to the team, and prepare for a "wrench" to be thrown into the middle of the interview that may change what they originally proposed. The "wrench" is meant to simulate the kind of improvised collaboration this person would experience on the team; it's a mini model of how folks in the room would work together. In the interview, the candidate presents their case and solves the wrench, as well as answers questions from the team. Project interviews should be paid since folks are doing original work for you. Offer an hourly rate or a flat fee. If budgets are tight, set a strict time limit and evaluate the work based on that projected timeline (rather than rewarding candidates who go over the time limit). Setting a time limit is part of accommodating for those who can't afford to spend hours and hours on an interview, like working parents, students, or candidates with multiple jobs.

- *Reference Checks:* At the end of Project Interviews, the Hiring Manager asks the candidate for two to three references. These references receive a note from either the Recruiter or the Hiring Manager that they will call for a fifteen-minute interview, where they plan to dig into the candidate's skills, previous working relationships, and biggest opportunities for growth. I like to use my reference checks as an opportunity to see whether candidates will be happy at my organization.

If you're wondering how many candidates you should see at each stage, my team has developed our own formula, which you will find along with a hiring scorecard at http://www.alidamirandawolff .com/bookreaders.

CREATE A HIRING COMMUNICATIONS PLAN

A Hiring Communications Plan serves as the single source of truth for promoting new roles. It captures the core messages candidates will receive, determines how internal teams and the community will receive information about the hiring process, and sets the strategy for communicating about hiring generally. While many organizations skip this step, it's very much a "first-minute" rather than "last-minute" solution. It's more work upfront that reduces the total amount of work during the hiring process overall. A Hiring Communications Plan also helps crystallize what people really need in a role, what will and won't be expected of candidates, and where sourcing gaps exist.

At Ethos, our plans vary from client to client, but they generally follow the same structure:

- *Overview:* What the plan is, who it's written for, and how they should use it.
- *Key Messages:* Two to three key messages we want candidates to take away from the role, as well as what messages our external partners and internal employees should know, repeat, and promote. Examples include: "We want to engage systematically marginalized groups to ensure that their voices are heard," and "The organization is investing in diversity, equity, inclusion, and belonging, and is taking steps to ensure an equitable search."[7]
- *Promotion:* This lays out thoughtfully and intentionally how you plan to reach candidates. We break out our promotions into categories.

    Announcements: Any social media, email campaigns, press releases, company blogs, event shoutouts, and prewritten copy announcing the role is open.

Partnerships: Who are our formal and informal partners? Who do we collaborate with? Our partnerships include the folks we work with to reach different communities, organizations with similar goals and audiences, and organizations we trust that are willing to publish, post, and promote on our behalf. In this section, we prewrite email messaging and promotional copy for them to share, along with our respectful call for their support.

Employee Outreach: All employees should know about open roles and should have the tools to communicate about them. As organizations grow more diverse, referrals actually become a positive when it comes to representation. Veterans Affairs activist and equitable hiring colleague Samuel Innocent has put it this way to me: "When companies ask me where they can find more veterans to recruit, I tell them to look at the veterans they have and ask them where they hang out, where they get their resources." Pre-write content for your employees to share and emphasize the importance of getting the message out to groups over specific individuals.

- *Job Boards:* Sixty-nine percent of job seekers find job opportunities through online job boards.[8] In our current climate, niche job boards seem to be the best option for employers seeking to diversify their candidate pool; unless they have succeeded at reaching a wide variety of audiences in their social media platforms, this is the best way to reach a different base of people.
- *Applications and Candidate Communications:* This allows for you to prewrite candidate messaging between each stage of the hiring process, from emails about the status of their application, rejection notices, and resource guides. Again, being thoughtful early allows for you to think about what a rejected candidate might need to

feel more supported (such as resources for other opportunities and links to guides), what an on-the-fence candidate would want to know about the organization (the organization's response to violence against communities of color or how remote work is assigned and put into practice, for instance), and why candidates should wait during a lengthier process ("We're being intentional to make sure everyone is given a fair chance" or "We have had 650 applications and we are carefully reading each one, including yours").

- *Internal Communications:* Keep employees informed. The amount of communication about hiring is up to you and your team's preferences; some teams hire so much a monthly summary is enough to keep them posted; others see a new hire as a major event and want to be kept up-to-date more frequently. This is the point where you determine your cadence and set your plan for how much to communicate.

- *Community Communications:* Chances are if your community is helping promote your roles, they also want to know what is happening with them. Just as you write a project management email for your employees, determine how you will do the same for your stakeholders. What will they want to know? How will they stay up to date? Who will keep them updated?

Once your Hiring Communication Plan is drafted, make sure you share it not only with the hiring team but other folks who can weigh in on tone, word choice, messaging, accessibility, and authenticity. Ask widely for feedback on what would make it clearer and more inclusive. Share those questions introduced at the beginning of this chapter with your readers and ask them for their input. What would eliminate "isms" in these communications? What biases might have translated into pieces of this plan?

Incorporate that feedback, and then bring the plan to life by conducting your announcements and outreach.

WRITE AND PUBLISH A JOB DESCRIPTION

The Hiring Communication Plan and Job Description typically come together at the same time, with the former representing the key messages to candidates and the latter factoring in the requirements of the role defined in the job description. The job description is essentially a blend of marketing material and informational guide for candidates.

In a heatmap-based study for LinkedIn's Talent Blog, Gregory Lewis found that 61 percent of candidates named compensation as the most important part of a job description and 49 percent said day-to-day responsibilities were the most important.[9] These findings suggested that effective job descriptions were clear and detailed about pay, benefits, and perks, and they laid out specific, performance-oriented goals that defined what success would look like. Less important were details about the organization itself, including vision, mission, and values. It's worth noting that optimizing job descriptions to prioritize the most relevant information can also help underrepresented and underserved groups. For example, since it's a well-studied phenomenon that woman-identified applicants are less likely to apply for roles when they do not meet most of the job description criteria (unlike their man-identified counterparts), focusing on the goals to achieve in the role rather than the qualifications to be considered for the role can help increase their likelihood of application.

Where you post, as described in the section on the Hiring Communications Plan section, plays a critical role in attracting a wider pool of applications. So does getting your job description right. It doesn't matter how many folks see it if they don't want to apply. To help you land on the job description that works best for you and your team, here is a template and a sample description.

A Job Description Template can be found at: http://www
.alidamirandawolff.com/bookreaders.

MEASURING FOR DIVERSITY IN THE APPLICATION PROCESS

Many businesses are afraid of the words "affirmative action." And based on our current climate, I understand.[10] On a regular basis, clients try to ask me if they should be using representation quotas without using the word "quota." I don't believe technical questions about how to move an organization in the direction of equity and inclusion should ever be taboo, so I am just going to spell it out. There is no way to know if you are reaching new pools of candidates or minimizing your bias in interviews if you do not set some sort of benchmark to measure yourself against. So, set the benchmark.

You must make sure you're using an Application Tracking System (ATS) that complies with the Equal Employment Opportunity Commission guidelines and tracks social identity as a means of helping an organization be EEOC-compliant. Never try to identify candidates based on what "you see." Ask for their self-identification information and make sure to provide "I do not wish to disclose" options.

- *Industry:* You can benchmark by representation in your industry, generally by pulling industry reports that show demographic breakdowns. There are two downsides to this approach. First, if your industry is struggling with diversity, you may be setting artificially low standards and congratulating yourself on a pool that is not diverse. Second, depending on your industry, there might not be a good data set.
- *Population:* At Ethos, we have come to prefer population data as a benchmark for candidates. Since we try to be representative of the communities we serve, not just for ourselves but in our client organizations, setting local

and national benchmarks helps us understand what it will take to look like our larger social environments. We typically prioritize local population data over national data for in-person roles and vice versa for remote ones.

- *Four-Fifths Rule:* In 1978, four government agencies (EEOC, Department of Labor, Department of Justice, and the Civil Service Commission) adopted a set of guidelines known as the Uniform Guidelines for Employee Selection Procedures. These procedures defined how to respond when a hiring process adversely impacted different groups and how to set identical standards to minimize this risk. They measured adverse impact by using the four-fifths rule—"a selection rate for any race, sex, or ethnic group which is less than four-fifths (or 80 percent) of the rate for the group with the highest rate will generally be regarded by the Federal enforcement agencies as evidence of adverse impact, while a greater than four-fifths rate will generally not be regarded by Federal enforcement agencies as evidence of adverse impact." You can set your benchmark around this rule when looking at an applicant pipeline. If on average 9 percent of White candidates advance from a group of 100 White applicants but only 3 percent of Black candidates advance from a group of eighty Black applicants, you would determine adverse impact since the group of Black applicants moving forward is less than four-fifths of the advancing White applicants.

EVALUATE APPLICATIONS

If you follow your Hiring Communications Plan and promote the newly developed job description accordingly, you should begin to see applications steadily arrive in your inbox or ATS. To evaluate applications, simply use your scorecard to measure for the competencies and values you determined earlier in the process.

With that said, it's often challenging to evaluate an application the same way you would an interview. I follow a few steps to make sure I am matching up to the scorecard appropriately and advancing candidates as fairly:

- Read the full application before scorecarding, highlighting any examples, metrics, or actions that could map to their experiences.
- Once you've read the application, match their answers to the questions on the scorecard first, then review their resume.
- Log notes on each scorecard dimension before assigning a score.
- How thorough is their application? Did they answer the prompts? Do you have a concrete sense of what they have done?
- Assign your scores.

PRE-INTERVIEW PERSONALITY ASSESSMENTS

I have worked with several organizations who love assessments like DiSC, Myers-Briggs Type Indicator (MBTI), and StrengthsFinder. I think these tools are invaluable resources for team development and team building, but I treat them all with apprehension in the hiring process. While requiring candidates to take personality assessments is not illegal, the tests themselves can be characterized as discriminatory, especially depending on how application screeners use them.

My general wariness toward personality assessments during the hiring process is best summed up by my experience with a prominent consumer packaged goods company. The leadership team had benefited immensely from executive coaching through the DiSC framework, and they decided it was time to introduce DiSC as part of their hiring process. Before candidates interviewed, they had to take DiSC. On more than one occasion, I listened to members of hiring teams say that while the candidate seemed more than qualified for the job, the organization "needed more D's and Di's, not S's." Candidates were neither consulted on their results[11] nor asked interview questions that would help contextualize their results. This assessment-based mechanism also helped legitimize bias. Why are "D's" and "Di's" more needed than "S's"?

At their core, personality assessments tell people what their preferences are, not *who* they are. However, in the often black-and-white, time-sensitive world of hiring, they are treated as shorthand for knowing everything about a person. This does not just reinforce biases about "kinds of people" and create a system of gatekeeping; it often strips organizations of opportunities to hire folks who they badly need. One of the most gifted managers I have ever worked with was hired for a role, but saw that role modified based on the personality assessment results. This particular assessment said she would not be a good manager because she was nonconfrontational and more focused on collaboration than results.[12] While the organization hired her, they stripped her of management responsibilities upon starting. She left after six months and went on to become one of Chicago's most sought-after people-management experts.

INTERVIEW CANDIDATES

Even if you follow the interviewing process you developed before posting the job description exactly to a tee, bias will still enter interviews. We are careful at Ethos never to promise to "eliminate bias" because we don't think it's possible; we do, however, believe in minimizing bias by naming what kinds are most likely to enter interviews and how to manage them. This involves both knowing

what common hiring biases are, as well as a team naming what you
are biased for and against.

COMMON HIRING BIASES AND HOW TO MINIMIZE THEM

Bias	Examples	Proactive Intervention
Halo Effect: The halo effect refers to attributing positive traits to people who feel affinity with or seem like you.	A candidate who dresses and speaks like you and supports your favorite team may seem like they have leadership tendencies.	Use your guiding questions and scorecard to determine if those leadership tendencies are actually there.
Horn Effect: Inversely, the horn effect involves unfairly judging someone who is different.	A candidate wearing your rival team's logo or sporting a tattoo of a band you dislike may seem like they wouldn't get along with your team members.	Always go back to the largest pool of data available to you and test it. What specific behaviors did they mention that triggered this belief they would not be collaborative? Can you tie those behaviors to examples? What were they?
Recency Bias: Recent events tend to weigh more heavily on our decisions than events in the past.	"All of our employees from the University of Pennsylvania are great with customers. This candidate went there, too."	Reread the job description. Where on the job description does it define that going to this university is a requirement? How are those employees tied to this job description? What do you know about why that candidate went to that school? And why other candidates didn't? Go back to your scorecard.
Conformity Bias: Group pressure around an opinion or decision that subconsciously determines how you evaluate a candidate.	Before completing your scorecards, you talk among yourselves as a hiring team, and one person emphasizes that the last candidate was clearly the strongest.	Always complete your scorecards before debriefing on candidates or interviews. Make sure you have documented your notes. Refer directly to your scores and notes when discussing candidates.
Confirmation Bias: The tendency to favor information that confirms already established beliefs.	"The candidate coming in this afternoon led two fundraisers last year. They're bound to be a phenomenal salesperson."	Here is where those pre-designed questions come into play; challenge your own assumptions and probe. Ask this candidate what they inherited on their team—did they already have a book of donors to call? Or did they have to build them from scratch? How was that situation different or similar to the one they would be navigating in your organization?

COMMON HIRING BIASES AND HOW TO MINIMIZE THEM		
Beauty Bias: The tendency to favor or disfavor candidates based on appearance.	A stylish, attractive candidate is evaluated as more "polished and presentable" than other candidates.	This one is especially insidious because perceptions of beauty are directly tied to social identity, with ability, body size and type, race and color, and gender all uncomfortably intersecting with what is considered "presentable." Lest I repeat myself, always stick to the questions and ask about specific scenarios, behaviors, and impacts.
Commitment Bias: The tendency to increase our commitment in a decision based on prior investments despite evidence that the cost of continuing down our current path is much greater than any expected benefit.	"We have been interviewing this person for three months. Okay, so we don't feel great about them. Shouldn't we just move forward? Think about all the time that's gone into this."	This is the sunk-cost fallacy at its finest. Remind yourself that firing someone is expensive, time-consuming, and hard. Hiring someone you think will fail can undermine other team members, hurt results, and impact morale. Better to call it part of the hiring process than to keep stringing someone along you will be betting against from day one.

As I shared earlier, I have a bias for profiles similar to mine. I also have a bias against people who talk slowly or go on tangents, don't lead with high energy, and speak in truisms or aphorisms. When we come together to review our scorecards, my team brings these up and challenges me to produce real evidence, rather than impressions, to support my statements. As you move through interviews it will be important to come to your own conclusions first, encapsulate them in scorecards, and then as a team share what came up for you. Scores, and specifically having minimum scores, helps this process enormously.

In particular, you score candidates and talk through together who will advance once you have collected information for yourself. Your colleagues may share their analyses to change your mind, especially focusing on introducing new information, but typically, consensus rules hold. Candidates move forward if folks agree or stand aside, but blocks are taken seriously, discussed, and addressed collectively.

It's important to note that after the first screen, email rejections are not acceptable. Always call candidates to let them know they are not advancing and show them respect and gratitude for the time they have invested in the process. Of course, you can always follow up thoughtful voicemails with emails.

CONDUCT REFERENCE CHECKS

Once the hiring team has decided on a candidate to make an offer to, I recommend the Recruiter or the Hiring Manager call their references within one to two days, using their predeveloped questions.

I am known for calling references and saying something along the lines of, "I know the reason you were listed as a reference is because you have glowing things to say about this person, and that you really care about them. Given everything you now know about me, the organization, and the role, do you think they would be happy here?" One reference for a candidate responded to this question with a "No." They said because they *did* care so much, I should know this person hates ambiguity and change, and it seems like they'd have to navigate a lot of it at my organization. In another instance, the reference told me the person I wanted to make the offer to wasn't actually very invested in DEIB and may burn out quickly. This was the same person who told me the candidate was the most brilliant mind they had ever seen.

MAKE AN OFFER

Most of the time, the references go well, which means moving to an offer is straightforward. Obviously keep your organization's policies, procedures, and protocols in mind. Additionally, take a few steps to maximize honesty, openness, accessibility, and transparency when you make an offer.

- Call the candidate to make the offer first. This will allow you to go over the contents of the letter, gauge any stopping points or roadblocks, and give the person more contextualized processing time. Make sure they also have the letter by the time the call is done.
- On the call, be crystal clear on why the candidate was chosen and what the offer includes.
- Give candidates the opportunity to ask questions and address the offer. Don't send the offer letter until it seems you're on the same page.
- It is likely you will have two exceptional candidates in your final-round stages, which means that if one declines the offer, you will have another to accept. You want to be respectful of this and set clear timelines for accepting or rejecting offers. Give candidates three to five business days to decide. And remember to offer extensions when candidates ask for them.

When the offer is accepted, I emphasize the importance of personally reaching out to candidates who made it into the final rounds but did not receive an offer. To decline these candidates, be kind, attentive, and truthful, and leave on as good terms as possible. You may end up hiring this person for something later, so don't close the door on future opportunities.

7

ONBOARDING[1]

It is a bizarre and unsettling feeling,
to exist in a liminal state between two realms,
unable to attain full access to one or the other.
—ZAINA ARAFAT

───── PRINCIPLE #7 ─────

Onboarding is such a crucial part of the employee
experience, especially for marginalized groups,
that it deserves its own special category.

Onboarding occupies a special place in the R2P2 model. In some situations, I characterize onboarding as a part of recruiting because it's a natural extension of making an offer and welcoming a new candidate into an organization. Yet, onboarding plays a disproportionate role in retention; whether employees stay at organizations and what their attitude is toward their leaders, colleagues, and customers is often shaped during this time.

A study from Gallup found that only 12 percent of employees strongly agreed their organizations onboarded them well.[2] Another study from BambooHR found that 17 percent of employees who are hired, leave in the first three months at a new job, while 30 percent leave in their first six months.[3] The link between onboarding and retention exists across a variety of studies and sources, including research by Glassdoor, which showed that a strong onboarding process improves retention of new employees by 82 percent.[4]

New employees who left early cited a need for clearer guidelines around responsibilities, more effective training, and various forms of social recognition from peers and leadership as factors that would have convinced them to stay. These reasons tie back to a need for better onboarding, which in an ideal situation helps employees clearly understand their goals in an organization, introduces them to teammates intra-team and cross-team, and equips them with the institutional knowledge and skills they need to do their jobs well.

The challenges employees face in onboarding can relate back to "The Path." According to Miller and Katz, taking a "sink-or-swim" approach to employees during the onboarding phase is a hallmark of the Exclusive Club, Passive Club, and Symbolic Differences phases, where employees succeed based on how much previous context they have, including how well they assimilate into the existing culture and develop relationships with people who can decode organizational practices and protocols. Of course, the folks who "swim" in a "sink or swim" environment tend to have the benefit of a swim coach, whether it's the person who referred them, someone they share affinity and similarity with, or even a set of inherited language to use, behaviors to adopt, and persuasion skills to try.

From a pure performance standpoint, "sink or swim" doesn't actually work to bring the best performers to the top. Talented people without the resources to learn in an organization will often fail. Perhaps the most common result of a "sink-or-swim" strategy is that while some diligent, resilient, and hardworking people will rise to the top, many equipped in the art of what Harry G. Frankfurt calls the "bull session" will too. As he puts it:

"Bullshit is unavoidable whenever circumstances require someone to talk without knowing what he is talking about. Thus, the production of bullshit is stimulated whenever a person's obligations or opportunities to speak about some topic exceed his knowledge of the facts that are relevant to that topic."[5]

In other words, a lack of onboarding can inadvertently promote the success of folks who know less and speak more. This is especially challenging for members of marginalized groups, who have traditionally learned that they are hired, promoted, and rewarded based on performance rather than potential, which makes them less likely to engage in the specific kind of impression management "sink-or-swim" systems require.

THE POWER OF ONBOARDING IN PRACTICE

In my first real job as a management consultant, I onboarded over the course of six months, mainly through a training program geared toward helping my cohort understand each practice. I received minimal training and support in my day-to-day responsibilities, but quite a bit of education and mentorship when it came to the big picture. I always regarded my onboarding experience as one of the better parts of coming into the company, even though I had significant issues with the culture that led me to leave early on. Every other onboarding experience was a non-experience. I went through anywhere from one day to one week of training, and most of the onboarding came down to office tours, desk and tech setup, and paperwork. I never thought much of this lack of structure; it seemed on me to figure things out. As a result, I worked longer hours, reached out to my own mentors and friends, and did a lot of reading. For the most part, this worked for me.

It wasn't until I became a manager that I realized how flawed this system was. For one, my onboarding went well because I maxed out my capacity, working evenings and weekends. I lived with an intense amount of stress around my own perceived underperformance, which also led me to work harder and more often. This approach also worked for me because of my own privileges; I had a prestigious education that taught me how to find answers and conduct thorough research, and while my network was small, my university alumni team was more than happy to put me in touch with people already succeeding in my industry. The inaccessibility of these privileges hit me when a newly hired colleague in my venture capital firm began to struggle. His work quality seemed to be declining, rather than improving. Having just started my self-study in DEIB, I began to notice some patterns: he was the youngest person on the team, a collaborative learner as opposed to an independent one, and the only person who had not been "inside" VC for at least a few years. The more I paid attention, the more I noticed gaps in his institutional knowledge and a general ambiguity in his role. When I brought these observations to my other colleagues, the response was simple: "You came in at about the same point in your career, and you figured everything out yourself."

I had seen the extra time my colleague was putting in, and also that the extra time wasn't adding up to better outcomes. There was nothing inherently wrong with him. He was motivated, committed, and earnest. He took feedback well. He just didn't have enough context or guidance to act appropriately on the feedback. His manager was considering termination. That's when it occurred to me that I could help. I asked both our managers if his management could be transferred over to me. I spent a few planning hours each day coming up with a strategy for improving his performance based on what I had seen. That strategy ended up being a ninety-day onboarding plan. My manager was skeptical; this person had been working at the company for six months. Wasn't it a little late for onboarding? Still, he had been promising *me* development opportunities, and saw this as a chance to communicate his investment in my growth. I moved forward with the onboarding plan.

Three months later my new direct report went from a "D" rating to a "B+" in his company evaluation. Six months later, I gave him the news that he was receiving a ten thousand dollar raise. The main reasons for this uptick in performance were that he needed more direction and got it, and also, that he needed consistent one-on-one's, training sessions, and clearly defined goals. In other words, proper onboarding.

ASSEMBLE YOUR ONBOARDING TEAM

Since learning my first lesson around the power of onboarding, I've largely taken what I implemented with my own team member and refined, organized, and streamlined that process across dozens of teams and organizations. I am proud to say the structure I developed, which I have termed "Learn-Build-Do" remains largely unchanged. What has changed, though, is my view of who should be involved in onboarding.

As a new manager I internalized the belief that to do my job well, I had to take on the work of management completely alone. Onboarding was a one-to-one experience between my direct report and me. In hindsight, this approach only worked because I was on a team of fewer than ten people and I only had three direct reports; in bigger companies with more people to manage, this is impractical and unfeasible.

As you assemble your onboarding plan for your new hires, think carefully about whom to include and what roles they will play. I generally earmark about five categories of people to support onboarding. All of these folks should be given access to onboarding materials before the new hire starts, and they should convene to talk about how and when they plan to help in order to better coordinate responsibilities:

- *Hiring Manager:* The primary source of direction, guidance, and leadership for onboarding employees. They set and communicate the vision for the role, architect and measure progress on goals, and meet regularly with new employees to help them understand how to navigate the organization, achieve milestones, and teach them about core elements of their roles. Quality over quantity matters with a Hiring Manager; as much as time together in the early days of onboarding is invaluable, a Hiring Manager who is detail-oriented, focused, attentive, and present when they *do* spend time with their new hires is better than one who is pulled in too many directions and finds themselves splitting attention between their phones and their employees.

- *Team Lead/ More Experienced Peer:* This person may come from a People Operations or HR team, the new hire's own team, or another team. What matters is that this person feels established enough in the organization to explain implicit rules and behaviors, conduct technical and role-specific tutorials and training, and serve as a knowledgeable-enough expert that the new hire can touch base with them on a daily basis to ask questions and receive answers.

- *Intra-Team Peers:* While organic relationships between team members will form, it's important that folks at the new hire's level are prepared for their onboarding and ready and willing to help. Intrateam peers understand how the team works, what strengths and gaps exist, and what the general working environment is like. They are the ones most likely to socially recognize the new person, contributing to a sense of belonging.

- *Cross-Team Peers:* This is the broadest category, and arguably the most important. To avoid siloes, establishing relationships across teams early is critical; it's also practical. Your new engineering hire will likely have to handle customer support tickets; your new marketer will have to understand sales metrics to build lead generation strategies; and your new analyst will have to understand who will be using their analysis and for what. Crossteam peers also create more of an opportunity to weave new hires into the fabric of an organization. If there are affinity groups or employee resource groups established, new hires should be directly introduced to their members. If other social groups exist, new hires may find camaraderie on them, but only if they know about them. These cross-team relationships are especially important because of the challenge of being an "only." For example, one new hire at a client organization was the first person identified as gender nonconforming on the team, but not in the company. Letting them know about the Genderqueer Slack channel, and the work the LGBTQIA2+ group was doing around gender identity helped them understand there was a community for them in the organization.

- *Cross-Department Mentor:* In VC, there's a cynical slogan about entrepreneurs from marginalized groups I often repeated: "overmentored and underfunded." I am wary of mentorship programs for underrepresented and underserved groups because they can be patronizing and more focused on the volunteers than those the program is designed to serve. More importantly, I see mentorship programs used as tools to absolve those who should be doing more for members of marginalized groups (such as promoting them, investing in them, and spending money on them). With that said, mentorship that is tied to helping employees achieve success and is on top of (rather than in lieu of) other resources and opportunities, can be professionally life changing. Especially during onboarding, having an "insider" who understands the organization and is explicitly focused on providing a more outside view on how things work can be the difference between feeling rooted and confident in a new role versus rudderless and confused. This person should be in senior leadership, and from a department not immediately connected to the new hire's to blend access and anonymity.

STRUCTURING YOUR NINETY-DAY ONBOARDING PLAN

Establishing a predefined, repeatable process for onboarding will reduce the amount of time you spend ramping up new hires and increase overall retention. During the first ninety days, your employees should progress from learning to doing; they should receive all necessary introductions, training, and education during this timeframe. To achieve this goal, I break up the ninety days over four phases:

- 1 Day: Defining Purpose
- 1–30 Days: Learn
- 31–60 Days: Build
- 61–90 Days: Do

Each new phase overlaps with and builds off the others. While an employee focuses on learning in the first thirty days, learning does not stop at the sixty- or ninety-day marks. However, where that employee expends energy shifts. At sixty days, they are still learning but spending more energy on building.

I advocate for a true ninety-day onboarding period because putting a container around activity helps new hires ease into a role, mentally prepare for their responsibilities, and develop the understanding and skills necessary to succeed. Ninety days also makes a new work environment more manageable. For new people joining teams, they don't just have one full-time job, but two: doing the job and adjusting to the culture and conditions of the job.

DEFINING PURPOSE

One of the most important phases in onboarding is often the most neglected: defining the new hire's purpose in the organization. This goes beyond a job description and starts with expectation-setting.

In *The Employee Experience*, researchers Tracy Maylett and Matthew Wride made a discovery about employee satisfaction. "Engagement, satisfaction, and happiness often depend less on the conditions in which one works and more on whether expectations are aligned and met." What matters is whether expectations are set around these factors when people start. Onboarding should start before an employee's first day, and in fact, usually starts during candidate interviews. Whomever you hire should have at least a general idea of:

- What am I here to do?
- What do I have at my disposal to do it?
- What do I need to know to succeed?
- Who are my key stakeholders?
- How am I being measured?
- What behaviors are rewarded in this culture?
- What behaviors are looked down upon in this culture?

Granted, the answers to the first five questions may change. Still, when you design the new role you should have the answers to these questions in mind. You should also be transparent about what could change and why, which will appropriately set expectations around the overall environment.

To truly define a new hire's purpose, work on developing guiding frames.

VISION STATEMENT

Not to be confused with the company's vision statement, this is a short paragraph defining the vision for the role. This paragraph should clearly state the overarching problem the person is being hired to solve or objectives they're expected to meet by clearly spelling out what they are there to do, how they will do it, and why it matters. What sets this statement apart from an overview in a job description is that it factors in the person you hired and the unique skills they bring to the table.

For example, while a job description might call for a creative director who elevates the company brand through exceptional storytelling, the vision statement for a new hire who specializes in design may specify exceptional visual storytelling.

ROLES AND RESPONSIBILITIES OVERVIEW

This document builds off the vision statement to clearly define the new hire's role and how that role will be met. The role consists of the three to five problems they will solve, while the responsibilities define how they will solve them.

In our creative director example, one of the bullet points under "Role" may be "Elevating the brand through exceptional visual storytelling," which could solve the problem of insufficient brand awareness in the market. Under "Responsibilities," however, the bullet point might say, "Architect Instagram strategy with an emphasis on original visual content."

GOALS

You absolutely must know how that person is going to be measured and communicate that in advance. Both developing a strategic plan for communications and building a base of 100,000 Instagram followers are goals. Before your hires even begin work, they should know what overarching value they're expected to drive in both quantitative and qualitative terms. However, you don't need to be exceedingly granular in putting these frames together; there's a time and place for that in the next steps.

USER MANUALS

User Manuals are bridge documents between the pre-onboarding and onboarding phases. In them, a new hire will answer five to seven questions about themselves that their direct manager and immediate teammates have also answered. I believe User Manuals are essential to running an equitable and inclusive onboarding process. Basically, they allow the new hire, the direct manager, peers, and mentors to demystify themselves *in their own words*. When done well, User Manuals allow folks to be upfront about who they are and what they prefer from day one, as opposed to engaging in an arduous journey of guesswork. They must be approached by all involved as new information meant to help folks adapt to one another and respond to preferences and needs. My go-to questions are:

- What's the best way to communicate with you?
- What's the best way to convince you to do something?
- What don't people know about you that you wish they did?
- What qualities do you most value in your teammates?
- What are some things people might misunderstand about you that you'd like to clarify?

- What most energizes you?
- What makes you feel most appreciated?

LEARN

In the first thirty days of onboarding, employees are measured by how much they are learning. It doesn't matter to me how fast your company is growing, how much is changing, or how many bodies in seats you need: employees need to learn to do the job to do it well. With that said, learning doesn't have to mean sending new hires to all-day lectures or training seminars. The 70:20:10 leadership development model suggests learning comes from 70 percent challenging projects, 20 percent coaching and mentorship, and 10 percent structured learning.

In other words, in those first thirty days, your new hires can spend 70 percent of their time working on hard projects the company needs solved. However, to do so successfully they need the coaching and mentoring, along with the structured learning, which usually takes on the form of training and tutorials. To create the optimal conditions for learning, build preparation and acceleration into onboarding.

PREPARATION

Preparation encompasses a huge amount of the onboarding process and sets the tone for the overall employee experience. This is where you provide all the tools, information, and connections needed for hires to truly acclimate.

In the preparation phase it's critical to make sure that on day one, new employees know where they're supposed to be, who they're supposed to meet with, and what they're supposed to do. Send all this information in a welcome email at least twenty-four hours before their first day.

When they start their first day, keep a checklist with you to make sure you're getting them what they need, from necessary equipment to a warm welcome from their peers and colleagues.

ONE-ON-ONES

Set up small, one-on-one meetings throughout the first month to welcome your hires into the organization, provide an overview of culture (what behaviors are celebrated, tolerated, and forbidden), set expectations around roles and responsibilities in more detail than in the purpose-setting phase.

More personal meeting settings create relationships without hampering the generation of new ideas. Chances are you brought new people in to foster innovation, so make sure you're not putting them in situations where pressure to conform outweighs the freedom to contribute perspectives.

ACCELERATION

In the first thirty days you want to accelerate learning as efficiently as possible. That often means combatting a bias toward action. As Michael D. Watkins warns in *The First 90 Days,* don't fall prey to action imperative. Defining the "what" and the "why" of the role is necessary to quickly surface the best "how." To accelerate learning in your hires, employ these targeted methods:

- *Discovery Meetings:* Arrange meetings with experts in areas new hires will touch, as well as some they won't. These informational meetings will educate them on how people approach problems across departments and disciplines, allowing them to avoid the "blank page" problem.
- *Business Training:* Whether you go heavy or light on training, there is one session that is absolutely critical to

accelerating learning. That's a business strategy overview meeting where you train employees on the business itself, company architecture, strategic and/or business plan, and market conditions. This training should be interactive and prompt participants to ask questions and contribute new ideas to demonstrate understanding.

- *Diversity, Equity, Inclusion, and Belonging Training:* Chances are that if you're reading this book, your organization has already gone through some DEIB, antiracism, gender equity, disability justice, LGBTQIA2+ rights, or upstander intervention training. Since developing a shared language around these issues is vital, make sure these trainings are delivered to new hires, too. Regardless of whether your organization has started DEIB education or not, I advocate for two kinds of training in the onboarding process around social identity. The first is something we call "Active Listening for DEIB" at Ethos, which is a session designed for all levels of understanding that shares how much harder it is to listen to folks who are not like us and teaches active listening techniques and the art of questioning to help foster connections across groups. The second is a short history of DEIB at the company: what has been done, who has led these efforts, where the organization plans to go in this area, and why. This context will prove necessary as new employees acclimate and start setting expectations.

- *Learning-Based Projects:* These encompass a broad set of categories, but generally comprise projects that involve job shadowing, collaboration with experienced employees, and research.

- *Reading:* Exposure to leadership and development books and industry- or function-specific reading will increase new employees' knowledge base while also adding structure to their learning. I create a new syllabus for every new hire I bring on, whether they're a full-time associate or a part-time intern. I also try to accommodate learning styles, accessibility requirements, and other needs tied to ability. Not every person can sit down and read a book; they may need an audiobook, an online course, or the material formatted or delivered in another form.

Throughout this phase, whatever projects your new hires work on, determine their success by how well they're learning, not how astonishing their results are. You want to privilege what Daniel Coyle, author of *The Talent Code,* terms "deep practice."

Deep practice is "struggling in certain targeted ways—operating at the edges of your ability, where you make mistakes." Encourage your new employees to take on hard projects and push themselves to find new solutions beyond what they've done in past roles. Reward their analysis and refinement of errors over the end product, and the end product will eventually be superior to what you could have imagined.

BUILD

Learning doesn't stop after the first thirty days. It continues in tandem with the act of building. In some ways, building is just an extension of learning, where you trust new employees to dig deeper into the responsibilities themselves and engage in more independent work. This phase is where they begin to build social ties, frameworks, and a collection of early wins to propel them into successful execution once onboarding is complete. In this thirty-day block, they should focus on strategy, development, and implementation.

STRATEGY

Once new hires get the information they need, they should engage formal compilation and review. Their notes from discovery meetings, readings, and research should become findings on which they start to base more nuanced assumptions, hypotheses, questions, and ideas about the business and the challenges they've been hired to tackle.

This generally looks like a market analysis presentation, marketing audit, or research review session with me. Employees take their sources, along with their own original thought, and present what they've learned in a sixty- to ninety-minute presentation, complete with a final section featuring core observations and recommendations for the future.

Based on this analysis, give the new employees the direction to develop a strategy to convert what they've learned into value for the organization. This usually takes the form of a strategic plan in the core functional area they've been hired to tackle first.

At this point, you should also encourage new employees to take what they've learned about the overall organization and develop a strategy for individual professional success, complete with goal-setting, skills-building requests, and more targeted asks for resources. Usually a one-pager that you review and discuss with them monthly, this framework keeps employees focused on their own personal growth as a means of growing the business.

DEVELOPMENT

Now that a strategy is set, new employees use it to develop solutions to problems or opportunities for growth in real life. Take our creative director, for example. As her strategy, she may architect a proposal for heightening brand awareness through visual storytelling complete with recommendations and steps to take, all based on her assorted findings. Then, she must develop ways to implement those recommendations.

She could create Instagram campaign mock-ups, work with copywriters on new platform language, explore other highly visual platforms, and compile a list of influencers who can tell these stories. With such products developed, she must test their effects. This could involve seeking input from both internal stakeholders and those outside influencers on her campaign mockups, creating a small test campaign on Instagram to measure performance, and creating content on another visually centered platform with a quantitative eye on initial engagement.

"Development" also encompasses relationships. At this stage, new hires should know their peers well enough to collaborate and ask for help, leverage discovery meetings into real relationships that persist after onboarding, and clearly understand their most important stakeholders. Depending on the role, this may mean spending more time outside the internal company network. What matters is that they are integrated into a trusted group of people who all impact their performance positively.

IMPLEMENTATION

Implementation takes those tests from development and expands their reach. This is where employees begin to execute against the responsibilities they were hired to fill. Notably, they might not yet fulfill all their responsibilities. The goal is to go deep rather than wide during onboarding because the lessons learned about the way the organization functions will lay the foundation for all future work. It's about getting it right, first.

That's why implementation is all about securing early wins. For our creative director, her role is much bigger than running Instagram campaigns. But in the beginning, implementing successful campaigns does achieve the objective of spreading brand awareness and elevating the company's market position. The same logic applies to any other quick wins in the first sixty days, which typically take the form of fast fixes, initial pilots, new programs, project ideas, and system updates. All are important, but they typically focus on one area or one problem that needs to be fixed.

Watching new hires implement their findings and strategies is also the best way to understand how they're performing and gain alignment on what their role needs to be and how they can move forward. Providing real-time feedback during implementation is necessary for onboarding, the best means of ensuring expectations are aligned, and just good management.

DO

In the final thirty-day block, new hires are empowered and expected to "do" more than anything else. They should be measured according to progress on their goals, and they should understand they will be judged on outcomes as much as thinking and process. Still, with just two months under their belts, forgive mistakes, but understand why they are being made.

In my experience, it's fine if new employees make mistakes based on lack of historical information, shaky skills with new systems or processes, or even lack of expertise in an area. The solution generally is just more time, especially to process everything they are learning. I pay the most attention when I see they don't follow company rules, disrespect stakeholders, turn in sloppy or late work, or fail to communicate appropriately around deadlines. In the case of missing expectations, take the time to understand what is happening before jumping to conclusions. Why was the work turned in late? Are they struggling with time management? Were deadlines not clearly communicated? If there are behavioral issues around communication, breaking company rules, or coming off as disrespectful, start by asking them how they perceive the situation. Why did they show up that way? What happened before, during, and after? What information didn't they have? From there, work together to find solutions.

"Do" should be the easiest and least complex block of the process. This is where employees focus on cultivating relationships and teams, graduating from quick wins to longer-term ones, engaging in more wide-ranging work, and undergoing a formal review to ensure they're on track.

At this point, employees do more than ask for help, they in turn are helpful. They earn their team's trust, and depending on the role, even build their own teams to oversee and manage. If the role involves external stakeholders such as partners or clients, this is when they begin managing them on their own.

EVALUATE

Whether you do quarterly, annual, or even real-time performance evaluations, the last step in onboarding is always evaluation. Create a scorecard if you don't have one already or want to use a different scorecard than the one you used for hiring and complete an assessment of performance over the last 90 days. Ask the employee to complete a self-assessment. Then compare notes in a candid conversation around performance.

The evaluation stage is where you look at strengths and opportunities for improvement while getting feedback from the employee. It's also where you recalibrate on goals going forward to make sure you are still aligned. If you are no longer aligned, reset expectations and explain why they've been reset.

Every phase of this onboarding process is focused on goals that buoy and uplift your organization, and on how you can best position your people to achieve them. Refine it, tweak it, replace some of it, or use it exactly. Just remember: this is all in service of growth and goals. Know what you're working toward and why it matters; and know what your people are working toward and why that matters, too. Success will follow.

RETENTION

How you're listening is how you develop a culture, and how
a community of people listens is what creates their culture.
—PAULINE OLIVEROS

———————— PRINCIPLE #8 ————————

*Retention is about anticipating employee needs,
especially the needs of those most likely to experience
exclusion and face discrimination. Good leaders have
an open-door policy; great leaders walk the halls.*

Workplace stress increases voluntary turnover by 50 percent, which means in addition to hurting a company's bottom line by impacting the quality of work, it also leads to churn.[1] Churn is expensive, both financially and culturally. The cost of replacing a single employee is anywhere from 20 percent to 50 percent of that person's annual salary, and the process often results in encouraging others to leave, too.[2]

So much of the conversation around retention in workplaces centers on developing more innovative strategies around project-based work and rotations, introducing new health and wellness perks, and offering attractive financial or social incentives to stay. I don't disagree with these strategies, but in my experience, the folks who develop them aren't spending enough time with their employees to understand what drives their departures.

Recently I conducted thirty-three research interviews for a client undergoing an intensive equity audit. Attrition was high across several departments, but remarkably low in others. I was trying to get to the bottom of this polarized retention trend, so I asked each respondent the same two questions: Why do people leave? And, why do *you* stay? The people who left were overwhelmingly identified as BIPOC and queer, and they had experienced discrimination. Those who didn't explicitly fall into this category left because of low pay and limited advancement opportunities. Interestingly, many of the people who stayed cited low pay, limited advancement opportunities, and discrimination against themselves and others, but still chose to continue working at the organization for anywhere from five to almost twenty years. For them, the pros outweighed the cons. Of the thirty respondents, every single one noted a major contributing factor to staying was they felt strongly bonded to their colleagues and peers. Respondents from the teams with the highest retention notably expanded on this answer by talking about how smart, thoughtful, caring, and kind their colleagues were. These respondents also cited working in roles where even though there was significant ambiguity and a "ceiling" to their potential for leadership and higher pay, the work itself was meaningful, challenging, and tied directly to their continuous learning.

What struck me was the contrast that emerged based on their responses. Retention was highest when people had fulfilling, gratifying, and enjoyable *day-to-day* experiences, even if they faced triggering or traumatic events and larger scale perceived indignities, like being paid "embarrassingly low salaries" or being "denied a management title even though I manage a team of four." To explore this idea further, I interviewed six employees who had left the organization in the past year. What I heard reinforced this contrast between the day-to-day and the more global-scale

happenings of an organization. Basically, employees did leave because of lack of benefits, low pay, and few opportunities for advancement, but *when* they chose to leave had more to do with
day-to-day experiences. The more disconnected they felt from
their peers, and the more they noted repeatable, commonplace,
and daily slights, the more motivated they felt to leave, even if
there was risk in a bad job market.

Anecdotally, this phenomenon rang a bell. Right after companies started responding to the murder of George Floyd, I chose to
open up office hours to leaders trying to navigate how to support
their Black employees *and* Black employees themselves. One person reached out to me directly. I had worked with this person for
several years as a partner and collaborator, and I found her to be
resilient, compassionate, and admirably forgiving of the many indignities she experienced as the only Black woman in executive
leadership in her organization. The day we spoke, though, her
orientation to her company was different. She explained that it
had been over a week, and not a single person had checked in to
ask how she was doing, even though her family was directly impacted by the events that preceded the protests. This opened her
eyes to the fact that on a *daily* basis, she checked in on others, but
never found this reciprocated. For her, the last straw came when
leaders on the team asked her to compile resources for supporting
the Black community. She approached the task with consideration
and care; even though she didn't feel like engaging with these issues before processing her own trauma, she took the initiative as a
means of making sure other employees felt seen and heard. After
she shared her recommendations with the leadership team, they
presented them to the company, without ever mentioning or cred-
iting her. She quit two weeks later. Despite being denied two pay
raises, being de facto demoted during an organizational restruc-
ture, and navigating a recruiting process where her colleagues routinely explained the lack of diversity as lack of talent in the Black
community, she had never considered quitting until then.

Day-to-day interactions shape the employee experience. While fair compensation, generous benefits, and career pathing significantly affect retention in the long term, many employees walk away from all three if they feel excluded, unsafe, and socially rejected. Since employees from marginalized groups are more likely to experience exclusion, they also tend to leave more frequently and in higher numbers. It's my belief that the reason the language of microaggressions has entered workplace vocabulary so quickly is because they happen daily and in small, subtle ways that create a kind of low-lying panic and dissatisfaction that ultimately becomes intolerable for underrepresented employees to bear.

In our current environment, the idea of the daily employee experience is even more important because of what is counted as workplace stress (and therefore addressed) and what is not. For as long as I can remember, workplace stress has meant overwork and the associated overload that goes along with it. Companies have not talked about stress in terms of factors like racial violence, gender-based violence, increased caretaking pressures, declining economic opportunities, and anxiety related to financial precarity, climate change, and the political environment. Consequently, employees experiencing these kinds of stressors are left to manage them alone, with no support, recourse, or even opportunity for discussion.

The solution, in my view, then, is to introduce retention strategies that consider day-to-day experience, especially in relation to social identity. The theory of small acts, which Daniel Coyle explores in *The Culture Code*, may serve as a better model for creating healthy social environments for all identities. Perhaps the best example of this idea comes up in his discussion of what makes people feel safe at work. Among the many examples he lists, a few stand out to me: profuse amounts of eye contact; frequent short, energetic exchanges (as opposed to long speeches); few interruptions; lots of questions; intensive and active listening; humor and laughter; and small, attentive courtesies like saying "thank you" regularly.[3] While these small acts may seem more organic than intentional, organizations can and do encourage these behaviors, especially during a team's formation.

INCLUSIVE TEAM-BUILDING EXPERIENCES

When Hollywood portrays corporate team building, the picture is often the same: trust falls, summer camp–inspired games, and intense competition. Team building tends to look like junior high, and depending on what you're watching, it's a very White, privileged experience. But that's not *all* team building is.

Team building is a kind of convening that focuses on fostering motivation, cooperation, and collaboration. Activities and exercises make up much of the core of team building, and depending on how well-designed and executed they are, they can bring teams closer together.

For inclusive team-building experiences, I tend to favor ones that prioritize cultural immersion,[4] which seeks to create learning opportunities and facilitate deeper connection points between people who don't normally interact with one another, while deepening understanding of different cultural identities.

Immersion can take place in the local community or even by bringing people into a company for a daylong program that allows teams to develop rapport and relationships with those unfamiliar to them. These initiatives focus on three stages of learning: priming, experience, and action. Put in context, I think of team-building work Ethos has done in collaboration with Upwardly Global, a national nonprofit that helps recent immigrants and refugees return to their professional fields in the United States through career coaching and corporate connections.

Together with another learning organization, Ignite Global, we designed a day-long immersion program where employees:

1. Came together to learn key terms around cultural identity and DEIB, as well as take turns sharing more about their own identities (priming)
2. Helped members of the Upwardly Global community, recent asylees looking for work in the US, practice networking chats and review resumes (experience)
3. Discussed what they learned together over dinner, focusing on putting together fourteen-day and thirty-day action plans to translate lessons into opportunities in the future (action)

BRINGING DIVERSE GROUPS TOGETHER

Affinity bias happens when we identify with those who are like us and go out of our way to help them. When we experience affinity bias, we don't deliberately act *against* those we don't share affinities with, but we don't invite them in, leading to feelings of exclusion and the development of cliques. "Intention" is an important word in DEIB because of phenomena like these; if we don't proactively seek to challenge the status quo, it shows up unexpectedly in ways that compromise our chances of change. To introduce more intention into our teams, we first must understand how groups develop naturally so that we can steer them with thoughtfulness and strategic thinking.

BRUCE TUCKMAN'S STAGES OF GROUP DEVELOPMENT[5]

In 1965, educational psychologist Bruce Tuckman was looking for a way to support development, motivation, and success in groups. As part of his research, he landed on a new model of understanding group development, also known as the forming-storming-norming-performing model.[6]

At each phase, the group underwent a different experience that shaped the way they worked together. The first two phases, forming and norming, can be characterized by a focus on individual versus group goals and a lack of trust. The second two phases shift from a focus on individual goals to group goals, a common language and set of guidelines for working together, and a greater sense of benefit of the doubt. Broken down further, these phases take on unique shapes of their own.

FORMING	STORMING	NORMING	PERFORMING
Group members come together for the first time. Together, they: • Ask questions and attempt to coordinate responsibilities • Socialize and engage in get-to-know-you behaviors • Behave professionally and politely, often sticking to safe topics • Prioritize their own goals over the goals of the group • Work independently and from a place of limited information	As group members learn more about one another and feel the pressure to sort the group out, they begin to: • Voice their opinions, which can lead to conflict, disagreement, and personality clashes • Start to establish hierarchies and roles, often resulting in competition, struggle, and lowered motivation • Navigate tensions as judgments come to the surface and individual goals come up against group goals	Group members resolve conflict and come to trust one another. They: • Become aware of competition and decide on a common goal • Resolve disagreements and personality clashes • Experience a sense of shared responsibility • Establish norms for working together • Come to accept one another for who they are • May return to sticking to safe topics to avoid clashes or disagreement	With norms established, group members focus on achieving common goals. They succeed when they: • Motivate one another • Empower team members to make decisions without supervision • Engage in healthy dissent and conflict that aligns with group norms • Participate at high levels and in equal measures

In this model, Tuckman emphasized that groups don't always move through the stages of group development in sequence. While all groups begin in the forming stage, some never graduate from forming to storming, others get stuck in the storming stage permanently before disbanding, and still others who make it into the performing stage revert back to other stages, especially storming. In order to use Tuckman's model to design your day-to-day behaviors, start by looking at a diverse group of people in your organization currently collaborating, especially one you belong to. What stage are you in? Why? Based on this model, what might need to happen to move you forward? Once you have determined your answers, ask other members of your group where you are and why. Use the composite results to develop a plan of action.

For example, if you determine you are in the "Forming" stage, a plan of action may look like going through the User Manuals exercise in chapter seven together and practicing a simple "I want" and "The group needs" exercise. In this exercise, each person takes turns naming what they want (their individual goal) and what the group needs (their perceived group goals). Based on the responses, you define a shared goal together, as well as a few rules of engagement that consider individual interests.

CHECKING IN BEFORE CHECKING ON

While Tuckman's stages can help groups that are already working together, it's clear that so much of the employee experience hinges not just on how well folks collaborate, but the bonds between them. As previously taboo topics shift into necessary workplace conversations because of social movements like Black Lives Matter, Me Too, Disability Visibility, and others, learning how to create different kinds of spaces for employees is critical to fostering healthy social environments. Part of creating those spaces is teaching *all* employees how to behave inside of them. For this reason, active listening, dialogue and resonance, and techniques rooted in compassion must become part of the fabric of an organization.

This starts with understanding what empathy is. As Leslie Jamison writes in *The Empathy Exams*, "Empathy isn't just remembering to say *that must be really hard*—it's figuring out how to bring difficulty into the light so it can be seen at all. Empathy isn't just listening, it's asking the questions whose answers will be listened to. Empathy requires inquiry as much as imagination. Empathy requires knowing you know nothing."[7]

Colleagues have to learn to avoid assumption and instead choose broad, non-leading questions geared toward heightening understanding. It's the difference between learning of another act of violence and responding with phrases like, "I am so sorry" and "I feel terrible about this; I can't believe it's happening," to asking questions like, "How are you, really?" and "Do you want to talk about what's happening in the world? Or, stick to work?" When folks respond, resonance statements like, "I hear you, and what lands with me is . . ." can help establish that sense of connection.

This kind of communication is in line with what Massella Dukuly, Leadership Trainer at LifeLabs Learning, terms "checking in before checking on." It's focused on being helpful, understanding, and nonprobing. The tendency, especially for folks in the dominant group, when trauma or tragedy enter the workplace orbit, is to seek information. But this can feel extractive if relationships don't exist between these folks and the ones most impacted. That's why establishing a regular check-in practice, one that exists outside of outrage, catastrophe, or trauma, is so valuable. Those "check-ins" allow for those whom you check in with to choose how they respond and what they share, as opposed to feeling like they *have* to explain because someone with power is asking.

UPSTANDER INTERVENTION

Early in my career, I picked up a piece of psychological wisdom that has never left me. We are often angrier with the people who were supposed to protect us from harm than the ones who harmed us. We expect those who cause harm to behave the way they do; we don't expect the people we trust to stand by and do nothing.

If employees stay in organizations because of their deep-rooted social bonds and leave when they feel an absence of them, it stands to reason that we have to teach people in our organizations to stand up for one another. And if we are going to insist employees "bring their full selves to work," we have to understand that those selves won't always be accepted or appreciated. In those cases, intervention is necessary for safety and security. Carole Mc-Donnell's work in the essay "Melchizedek's Three Rings," featured in *Nobody Passes: Rejecting the Rules of Gender and Conformity*, sums this idea up concisely: "The ideal of open-mindedness only works when we know we have nearby allies who will stand up for us." We also have to understand that when that harm comes, the same leaders and members of the People team *can't* uniformly come to the aid of those impacted; it's not logistically feasible. Employees have to have the tools to advocate for one another.

At Ethos, we think the tools for advocacy start with a very basic technique that some may know as "bystander intervention," but we label "upstander intervention."[8] The Four "Ds" of upstander intervention are simple:

1. *Direct:* The "D" most people are familiar with, "direct" involves stepping in and directly intervening in the moment.
2. *Distract:* Change the subject, remove the person at risk or being harmed from the situation, or generally create a distraction. "Distract" is a short-term solution

that works best in scenarios where folks will not be encountering one another again. In workplaces, it's best used in combination with other Ds.

3. *Delegate:* Escalate a situation to an authority figure. Many employees default to reporting what took place to HR or a direct manager. While this can be a valid response, "delegate" may also mean turning a group into an authority figure by convening others and mobilizing them to put social pressure on the person doing harm to change.

4. *Delay:* Check in with the person harmed after the fact, offering help and support. Not all practitioners make this an option, but I think it's essential in workplaces where folks may not have been there, were distracted by other factors in the moment, or didn't fully have context until afterward because they were new to the situation.

The power in this model is that it gives employees options for how to respond when they witness a microaggression or an act of discrimination. Since fear of conflict and not knowing what to do in the face of conflict is the number one reason employees don't act, we try to eliminate this challenge by giving them practical models to apply. In our experience, the Ds are helpful, but they are only used when employees can see what they look like in real-life situations. Here are a few common microaggressions, including what they're called, what they look like, what message they send to the receiver. Based on what you've now learned about the 4Ds, take a moment to consider which Ds you would apply and how to each situation.

THEME	DESCRIPTION	HIDDEN MESSAGE
Ascription of Intelligence	Assuming lesser intelligence (or in the case of certain groups, fetishizing a kind of intelligence, like math skills) based on social identity. *To a Black person: "You're so articulate!"* *To a Latinx or Asian American person: "Your English is so good!"*	BIPOC people and immigrants aren't generally as intelligent or well spoken as White people. "You are an exception. I assumed you would not be."
Color Blindness	Denying the experiences of BIPOC people by questioning the credibility and validity of their stories. *"There is only one race, the human race."*	Assimilate into the dominant culture. Don't talk about how you have been marginalized. Don't identify by your social identity.
Myth of Meritocracy	Using the idea of meritocracy to explain away a lack of diversity and opportunity for people from marginalized groups. *In response to someone pointing out a lack of diversity in the candidate pool: "I believe the most qualified person should get the job."*	The playing field is even so if you can't make it, the problem is with you. People from marginalized groups would succeed if they worked harder; there aren't barriers to their success other than themselves.

I recognize that there are multiple possibilities in addressing these scenarios and depending on your own relationships to power, you may need to take a different approach. For example, in response to, "There is only one race, the human race," I would use a direct intervention. I might say something along the lines of: "I hear you. I think you're trying to say we're all in this together. And the way that lands on me is that saying the real racial experiences our colleagues are going through aren't real. I don't think this is what you mean, so I want to call it out to make sure.

I want to make sure our peers aren't in situations where they feel invalidated." In this scenario, I would either be a DEIB consultant or the CEO of the company; I am also a White person. There would be no major consequences for me in sharing this perspective, and most likely, the person would have to listen because of the power dynamics of the situation.

Of course, what the 4D's don't address is how to check your own biases. For that, I like to use an organizational development tool that I find applies nicely to DEIB: the Ladder of Inference.

A description of the Ladder of Inference can be found at: http://www.alidamirandawolff.com/bookreaders.

BECOMING A LEARNING COMMUNITY

By this point, it's probably apparent to you that to engage in the team development retention strategies critical for an environment focused on belonging, learning is necessary. This is an easy sell. Even the most resistant clients agree that training would be a good solution. But at the risk of undermining half of my business, the truth is that training isn't *always* a good solution.

That's because learning and training are not the same. Some learning can be achieved through training, but learning happens in a lot of different places and in a lot of different ways. Where it happens the most often and successfully is in organizations that have taken the time to develop learning communities where employees encourage one another to become more capable in their roles, coach one another on how to improve, and create the conditions for the pursuit of truth. If we go back to the example of the organization with the unequal attrition rates across departments, a key theme was that the teams where employees stayed offered opportunities for continuous learning.

To build a learning community, the organization has to decide on what everyone needs to learn. This should come from both an understanding of how the business operates, where it's going, and what it's trying to do, as well as what employees identify as their gaps and interests. Curriculum-building, in my opinion, should always involve the people who will be on the receiving end of the curriculum. Once the organization determines what employees need to learn, the process of designing that learning for multiple processing styles, levels of experience and familiarity, different roles, responsibilities, and power dynamics, and logistical concerns around availability, capacity, and delivery begins. It's worth noting that you have so many options to choose from when it comes to different learning methods. Here is an incomplete list:

- Prerecorded online video tutorials.
- Live training.
- Online simulations.
- Book clubs and reading assignments.
- Service learning.
- Project-based learning.
- Employee-led learnings, including but not limited to: Lunch and Learns, Speaker Events, Courageous Conversations, Brave Spaces, and healing circles.
- External career accelerators.
- Internal career accelerators.
- Mentorship programs.
- Peer coaching.
- Executive coaching.
- Team coaching.
- Forums and curated roundtable discussions.
- Lightning talks.
- Asynchronous wiki-based learning.

The list goes on and on. In the following pages I will provide a few examples for fostering both group learning and individual learning outcomes. The aim is to give you models to react against so you might develop your own.

DESIGNING A GROUP LEARNING PROGRAM

In *Powerful*, former Netflix leader Patty McCord emphasizes that organizations overtrain their employees in soft skills and dramatically undertrain them in understanding the organization itself. While I tend to agree, I also recognize that the makeup of your workforce determines how much soft skills training they need; this observation is true in an organization like Netflix that employs a strategy geared toward hiring more experienced people at higher compensation rates; it does not necessarily hold in organizations where employees are newer to the workforce or the industry and tools like emotional self-regulation, active listening, giving and receiving feedback, and stress management do not yet have a place in their respective arsenals. Designing a group learning program starts with understanding the group: Who are they? Are they at different levels of experience? How much individual or team-related training do they receive? What is their exposure to the overall business? The industry? The working world?

Once you understand the answers to these questions, you can begin categorizing groups of people in your organization and determining what they need to learn. Generally speaking, *how much* people need to go through structured training comes down to their role in the organization. The folks who need the most training are new—new employees, new managers, new executives. After that, the groups who need continuous learning, but perhaps in a more forum-like setting, are the ones who have the most ambiguous responsibilities. At our client organizations, these tend to be people managers.

Regardless of what level employees are in the organization, I believe the first place to start with any group learning program is to understand how well informed they are on the business. Since social relationships often determine access to information, this becomes a critical diagnostic of how equitable an organization is. Knowledge of power, and those with power already typically distribute knowledge among each other more than with those who don't have power. I like Patty McCord's measure around how well informed employees are.

If you stop any employee, at any level of the company . . . and ask what the five most important things the company is working on for the next six months, that person will be able to tell you, rapid fire, one, two, three, four, five, ideally using the same words you've used in your communications to the staff, and, if they're really good, in the same order.[9]

As you design your group learning plan, ask yourself: "What is my organization's official Way? What are our top five goals for the next six months? How do we like to do things here? How do our different business units work? What do we need to achieve to grow and succeed?" This is the backbone of your overall learning plan, even if most of the programs you plan to build hinge on diversity, equity, inclusion, and belonging. Relevance is key to adult learning; if employees cannot apply what they learned immediately to their day-to-day working lives, they will not use it. Every part of your curriculum should tie back to your organization's vision, goals, and expectations of employees, both implicit and explicit.

With this in mind, you can design your core plan. I recommend breaking the plan into four categories:

1. *New Employees:* With this group, more formal training is required, meaning less discussion and more content. They should learn as much about the company, the role they are fulfilling, and soft skills that will help them succeed. For example, if accountability is your organization's most deeply held value, then all new employees should be trained on what it means *at your*

organization, how it shows up in practice, and tools for holding themselves and others accountable.

2. *All Employees:* I am always cautious about overtraining employees, so for this group, I typically recommend no more than four formal training sessions in a category per year. That means you might lead four DEIB training sessions and four skills-based training sessions in the same year. Outside of regular formal learning, all employees should learn how the business operates and where it's going, which can happen through All-Hands meetings, Board Meeting share-out's, department spotlights, and internal wiki pages. More than that, and training fatigue sets in.

3. *People Managers:* People Managers, especially ones who have never been through formal management training, need it. It was about two years ago that I had this big lightbulb moment: our organizations were getting the absolute best DEIB education I had seen in terms of rigor, complexity, and nuance, but change just wasn't happening. The reason was not lack of interest or resistance; managers just didn't know how to be managers, and much of what needed to change depended on how they led their teams. For People Managers, then, I advocate for cohort-based learning where they go through a four-to-six-month program geared toward not only learning new skills, but workshopping them in forums and on their teams.

4. *Executive Leadership:* Executive Leaders are an interesting group because they typically require less training, but more learning overall. That is, the learning plan built around this group should budget ample time for quarterly learning sessions led by department heads, monthly peer coaching forums around how to promote better outcomes among and across teams,

industry-specific learning for the purposes of innovation, and of course, personal development in the form of executive coaching and leadership development. Executive leaders should also be the guinea pigs for new learning programs; DEIB training must start with this group, which should be the most informed in the organization.[10] The same is true for core skills. Executive leaders are the models for their employees; if they can't manage their stress or demonstrate adaptability, it sets a negative precedent for everyone else.

Regardless of which group you are designing learning for, it's important to remember that what matters most is how folks engage in learning. I believe in a one-thirds model for all formal training. That means my sessions are broken down into one-third new content, one-third small group exercises, and one-third large group discussion. Adult learners need practice and processing time, usually with one another. Straight presentation formats rarely work for me. I also don't suggest making training mandatory, but instead use the power of social cues and norms to facilitate engagement. If you need this learning to do your job, you are likely to do it. If your leaders will be there, you will want to attend. If you know the experience will be interesting, inspirational, or informative, you will make the space in your schedule to participate. If you see this as an opportunity to bond with teammates you will be more inclined to be fully present.

A sample DEIB Training Plan can be found at: http://www.alidamirandawolff.com/bookreaders.

AFFINITY GROUPS[11]

When I launched Ethos, I never imagined I would spend up to half my time collaborating with companies on their affinity groups. In 2020, it seemed like overnight, every company I met with was either about to launch or had just launched their own DEIB affinity group. Overwhelmingly, our clients handed me an ambiguous brief that could be distilled down to a simple and lofty goal: enhance the impact affinity groups have in the company. But why? Answers ranged from the good ("We want to give employees a space to share their experiences and enact strategies to uplift people from underrepresented groups at the company"), to the bad ("It seems like it's the thing to do now"), to the cringeworthy ("We think if employees are going to complain about problems, they should be ones to deal with them").

I live by the words of the iconic Solange, namely "do nothing without intention," and in these groups, which also include employee resource groups (ERGs), business resource groups (BRGs), and diversity, equity, inclusion, and belonging committees, I saw an opportunity to launch grassroots initiatives that supported belonging in organizations. When done well, DEIB affinity groups have an enormous impact because they a) create a support system for folks who need a designated space to share their experiences, b) offer a platform for raising and addressing DEIB-related issues, c) provide the authority and resources employees need to take action on those issues, and d) build bridges between employees who would never have connected or learned from one another otherwise.

That begs the question: what does "an affinity group done well" look like in practice? Here are a few examples:

- *Diversity Recruiting:* At one organization, the DEIB Committee identified that most of the company was made up of Gen X and Boomer employees, with less than 10 percent coming from younger generational cohorts, because of a stringent experience requirement. They noted that this lack of diversity in generational cohorts also fed into a lack of diversity in other areas, since there had been a more recent surge in BIPOC and queer-identified STEM graduates in the last few years. To achieve their agreed upon vision of closing the opportunity gap in tech, a subset of committee members designed, developed, and launched an Apprenticeship program that fed directly into associate-level roles in software engineering, product and UI/UX design, and data engineering.

- *Equitable Promotion:* In another organization, individuals were more than two times as likely to become managers if they played in bands with other managers. This was a company that had gone from a handful of employees to hundreds in eighteen months, which meant that institutional knowledge was not common knowledge, and what clique you belonged to determined your access to information. Since so many of the current managers were partly promoted because of their close relationships with other managers—who happened to be their bandmates—employees outside of these tightknit circles didn't know about new internal opportunities. Members of the newly formed racial equity affinity group identified that this situation led to a relatively homogenous management layer despite the company's overall diversity. To create more opportunity for employees, its members partnered with the engineering team to build an intranet that posted open internal roles so that everyone could find out about opportunities. They also trained managers to truly interview internal candidates, rather than going off existing relationships or gut feelings. The next three promotions were awarded to people who did not play in existing company bands: two BIPOC men and one White gender-nonconforming person.

- *Company-Wide Appreciation:* Finally, at a publicly traded organization, the PRIDE committee teamed up with a broad range of other affinity groups to run microawareness campaigns in the office around special emphasis periods, including PRIDE and Black History Month. The committee members gathered stories of people, places, and events significant to the special emphasis social identity and created information placards in each conference room and public space about them. It created moments to engage with the microcontent before the start of a meeting and promoted awareness around the office of historical figures, moments, and movements *and* the employees who had shared their significance. People from across the organization would congregate around an image of James Baldwin or Grace Lee Boggs in the elevator bank and trade anecdotes and information, which deepened existing relationships and supported the development of new ones. Plus, in the free response section of the quarterly employee engagement survey, a majority of employees noted feeling more appreciated in a tangible way because of the initiative, specifically because it asked for their perspectives and created an ongoing platform to share them.

So, what did these initiatives have in common, besides clearly impacting employees and committee members in positive ways? First, each group featured and clearly defined one problem and sought out a clear solution that was both relevant and manageable for a group of people juggling other responsibilities. Second, each group time-boxed their scopes, focusing on projects that could be completed with a concrete outcome. Finally, they involved a broad swath of people in their process from start to finish.

As you're reading this, you might ask: "What do *I* need to do to make sure my company's group makes a real impact?" My answer, predictably, comes down to process. Who doesn't love a multistep process?

STEP 1:
IDENTIFY A COMPANY-SPECIFIC WHY

Whether you're a C-suite leader who is trying to inspire employees to take action around diversity, equity, inclusion, and belonging, or a change agent working to convince both leaders and peers alike that an affinity group is essential, the place to start is "Why does your company need an affinity group?" Before launching an affinity group, ask yourself these key questions to shape your perspective:

- What are the company's vision, values, and mission? How do these intersect with diversity, equity, inclusion, and belonging?
- What is your company's orientation toward diversity, equity, inclusion, belonging?
- How would an affinity group impact the company's vision, values, and mission? How would it support diversity, equity, inclusion, belonging at the company?
- Why is now the right time to launch an affinity group at the company?
- Who in the company will benefit from an affinity group? Why?
- How will the company know the affinity group is positively impacting the company? (Examples may include employee engagement scores and more representation in leadership.)

Ultimately, affinity groups are company sponsored, and without reciprocal commitments from both employees and the leaders of the company, they can't achieve their full potential. That's why it's critical to start with a vision that ties back to the organization's goals. This is true even if your affinity group already exists; while this step feels basic and rudimentary, it often gets skipped in the group's original formation (or the answers to these questions have changed over time).

STEP 2:
GET CLEAR ON RESOURCES, COMMITMENTS, AND EXPECTATIONS

Once you have developed a company-specific why, it's time to get clear on what you need to actually launch the group and who is in a position to provide it. This means identifying:

- *Who are your key stakeholders?* One of the challenging aspects of affinity groups is that you typically have at least two kinds: the people the affinity group serves and the people who empower the affinity group to serve them. Can you name these people? What do you need from them in order to successfully launch the affinity group?
- *What might you need to achieve the business case around the affinity group you've identified?* You might need money, time, leadership's public endorsement and participation, access to information, connections to other affinity group leaders, or even an external facilitator to support your initiatives.
- *For those you plan to involve in the affinity group, what do you expect them to commit?* Whether you are interested in creating a formal board for the affinity group or simply welcoming members, you need to know how you want them to commit to the group. Will you need regular meetings? Availability after hours? Do you want them to commit to surfacing new ideas and developing new

processes? What is your commitment to them? If they give you an hour a week for a full year, plus extra hours for launching one or two key initiatives, what will you commit to in supporting them? Will they have more access to professional development opportunities or a clearer conduit to the leadership team? Will you build team bonding and socialization into your structure? Knowing what you want others to promise and what you plan to promise in return is critical to identifying what resources you need.

- *Will you be compensating the members of the affinity group for their time?* If you don't plan on compensating employees, commitments to the group have to be crystal clear, as do other incentives. They will also need approval from their managers to allocate hours to the affinity group. If you do plan on compensating employees, you must agree on a structure that is tied to clearly defined roles and responsibilities and payment guidelines. I recommend a quarterly stipend system, where a project brief is developed for the group, and folks within the group are compensated accordingly (the same way you would compensate external consultants). Other organizations engage in bonuses and universal hourly rates for the extra time logged. In both of these cases, you will need a clear measurement and tracking system to make sure people are doing the work they are being paid for at equal levels, so as not to create divisions within the affinity group around pay.

- *What do you expect of the company, and what does the company expect of you?* Like the folks who end up participating in the group, it's important to lay out what you expect of those leading the company and what they expect of the group itself from the very beginning. Perhaps the most challenging issue Ethos works to solve when rebooting affinity groups is expectations misalignment between group members and the company's leaders. For example, if company leaders want the affinity group to be a way of educating employees on diversity, equity, inclusion, and belonging or social identity, but group members want a platform for activism, it's important to know that up front. It's also important to understand what employees expect and envision, especially if the affinity group exists to serve specific coalitions such as Gender Identity/Expression, Race/Color, Nationality/Ethnicity, and Ability.

STEP 3:
DESIGN AN INCLUSIVE PROCESS

The three most important parts of designing an inclusive process for launching an affinity group are to know your audience, clarify and contextualize, and create multiple entry points.

Know Your Audience: Design a process that reflects how your company likes to engage in projects and groups like this one. For example, if your company is remote-forward, make sure you build a Communication Plan for sharing information about joining the affinity group with folks who are remote and ones who aren't. As you design the process for actually getting your group together, make decisions on how people can participate in the group based on a few questions:

- How do people in the company best receive information?
- How do people in the company typically volunteer to participate?
- Who most often gets a voice? Who doesn't? How might you bridge that gap and make sure everyone has the chance to speak up?

- When has a group come together really successfully within the organization? What did that process look like?
- When did a group fail to get started within the organization? What did that process look like?
- Are the people the affinity group exists to serve helping design the application and/or appointment process?
- Who can you involve in the process to make it more inclusive?

Clarify and Contextualize: When you design the process for getting the group together, whether it's through soliciting applications, assembling an advisory committee to make special appointments, or a blend of the two, it's important to define how people join the affinity group, why this is the process, and what is expected of prospective participants and selectors. Write all this up in a Context Document, which gets shared across the company. Break down everything in the Context Document in an email, on a communication platform, and in a company-wide meeting.

Create Multiple Entry Points: My favorite moment in *Girl, Woman, Other* by Bernardine Evaristo is when one of the characters considers, "Why should he carry the burden of representation when it will only hold him back?"

I often see people take shortcuts in forming affinity groups. An organizer or company leader will suggest that a specific person from an underrepresented or underserved group should take this work on, whether this person is the only Hawaiian native in the company, one of the few openly gay salespeople, or otherwise. This is not the right approach. Running an affinity group is work, and to ask a someone to do this work when they haven't volunteered because of their membership in a marginalized group further marginalizes them, sends the message that bias and discrimination are their problems and not the company's, and asks them to invest time, effort, and energy in something they might not even care about.

Instead of taking this approach, I recommend acknowledging that an affinity group made up solely of allies will have gaps in our understanding, and it's important to name that within the company. Basically, market the opportunity to join, but also recognize that it's not the only way for the group to form or for others to benefit from the work.

Additionally, go talk to the people you want to advocate for. They may not want to join, but they may be open to talking about their experience and how to make it better. Invite the people you want to support, and gracefully accept if they decline while creating other avenues for them to share knowledge.

This advice goes for employees from dominant groups, too. Letting people know they can support and participate even if they don't join is critical to the process of building a relationship to the larger employee base.

STEP 4:
INVEST IN TEAM DEVELOPMENT IN THE FORMING STAGE

In my experience, this is the most critical step and the most overlooked. When new groups come together, they enter Bruce Tuckman's Stages of Group Development. When these groups try to skip the important process of getting to know each other's communication styles, bonding over shared experiences, and simply navigating boundaries, they struggle with performance and end up in the storming phase more often than not.

To get off the ground, it's important the group takes time to get to know each other. I recommend scheduling at least one "get to know you" lunch, using a straightforward assessment like the Four Tendencies or the MBTI-based Sixteen Personalities to identify working style preferences, and user manuals to make understanding one another easier and faster.

STEP 5:
DEVELOP A VISION STATEMENT

There may be a temptation at this stage to create the company's DEIB Statement if one doesn't exist already. While this may be a useful initiative in the future, it should come into being after you understand your affinity group's role in the organization. Depending on what you determine, you may find your group shouldn't touch the DEIB Statement or that the group has an obligation not only to create it, but to own it as well.

So, what goes in your affinity group's vision statement?

Vision: This is a paragraph or two about why your affinity group exists. This may echo the business case you built in step one, though it will likely be broader and higher level in order to encompass all the voices the group represents. Here is the opening of a vision statement I wrote recently: *"Our product is our people, and we believe that by creating the structures that allow every person here to feel welcomed, valued, and fully leveraged for who they are, we are supporting the growth of the company, our teams, and individuals from all backgrounds."*

Guiding Principles: If your vision is your why, then your guiding principles are your how. How do you plan to achieve your vision? What principles will you hold yourselves to? Some principles might include:

- "We believe in radical inclusion when it comes to decision-making."
- "We make the implicit explicit."
- "Research guides our initiatives."

Note that some of these principles speak to you and others don't. I highly recommend focusing on the guiding principles that resonate within your affinity group, so long as they align with or complement general company values.

Focus Areas: Your focus areas are the outcomes, initiatives, and products of your vision and guiding principles. Call them pillars or practices; all that matters is that they clearly define your scope. If your focus areas are education and community-building, you know that creating a public education program is within your reach. On the other hand, teaming up with HR to conduct a payroll audit to measure wage equity might not be. This offers clarity and helps narrow down infinite possibilities so you can direct your attention where it counts.

STEP 6:
SET MEASURABLE OBJECTIVES

This step is tricky because I always want to introduce it before setting a vision, so I am going to present both the pros and cons of setting it where I have.

Keeping affinity group members excited is 80 percent of the work. No exaggeration. Launching something new takes a big upfront investment. When we begin with objectives in our client systems, we have a facilitated brainstorm session where everyone gets to voice their highest hopes. They emerge motivated, excited, and ready to get to work because their internal drivers for change are being heard. This energy is infectious.

However, there are a few reasons why I'm putting this step after visioning. First, it's hard to set measurable objectives when you don't yet know who you are as a group. The objectives end up shifting in flavor, cadence, and order much more when they are set before the vision and pillars. There also tend to be more of them, and the group falls victim to overcommitment and lack of focus. Finally, at these critical early stages, when we've started with objectives, we've run the risk of having individuals commit more fully to the ideas they volunteered than to what the group ultimately decides will most positively impact others. This competition derails progress.

You may have noticed that I used the word "measurable" instead of just recommending "set objectives." To the earlier point of keeping people motivated, knowing whether efforts are working isn't just vital to building the business case and gaining continued support from everyone in the company, it's also what makes group members feel like they're contributing. A measurable objective can be assigned a specific number or an outcome. The point is that everyone in the group should know whether the objective is a) done and b) successful or not. Bonus points if each person in the group is assigned their own measure that they are responsible for tracking, reporting, and hitting over time.

STEP 7:
COMMUNICATE PROGRESS TO THE COMPANY

Once you have your vision statement and objectives in place, it's time to communicate what you've developed. For one, you now represent employees in a unique way, which makes you responsible for telling them what you are doing. Second, this is hard work, and it's often thankless. Burnout in affinity groups is common, and it's not just because of members' competing priorities doing core work.

Affinity groups that have impact typically do a lot behind the scenes, only to hear silence when things go well and criticism when things go wrong. Plus, as representatives of DEIB at the company, employees have expectations of you, whether you know them or not. To get a better sense of what these expectations are, take a pause to make sure you're meeting them, and create more opportunities for congratulations over corrections, continuously communicate what you are doing to the company.

STEP 8:
DEVELOP A ROADMAP AND ACTION PLAN

By now, you have the company's buy-in, your fellow employees know what you're doing, and you have a list of objectives you want to pursue. You're almost ready to get to work; all you need to do is map out the next three to twelve months. But how do you know what to do first and what to do later?

Start by looking at your objectives and determining if they are fully formed or need corresponding initiatives. Sometimes an objective is made up of three or four parts, each representing a whole development and rollout process. Make sure you know this ahead of time whenever possible.

Then, with your objectives and initiatives laid out, start ranking them based on:

- How long they will take.
- Whom they will impact.
- How much impact they will have.
- Who will lead them.
- What resources are necessary to launch them.
- Who needs to be on board to launch them.
- How much work it will take to maintain them over time.

With this in mind, determine which should be short-term (launching in zero to three months), midterm (three to six months), and long-term (six to twelve months). Lay them out in a timeline or roadmap format. From there, for each initiative, detail the steps necessary to achieve them as precisely and tactically as possible. These bullet points will form your action plan for the next year.

Remember quality over quantity is absolutely critical when it comes to affinity groups. Choose no more than one to two objectives to pursue per time frame to avoid overwhelming group members and leaving loose ends.

STEP 9:
PRESENT THE ROADMAP
AND ACTION PLAN TO THE COMPANY

Once the group has agreed on the Roadmap and developed the Action Plan, it's time to share it with key stakeholders. Depending on where you work, this could be your affinity group's sponsor, the leadership team, or even the whole company.

Following the guidelines in Step 7, make sure that that the information is available in multiple different formats, and create a few different opportunities to engage with feedback so that you can make adjustments, revisions, and additions based on the responses you receive.

STEP 10:
LAUNCH THE FIRST INITIATIVE(S)

To quote one of my favorite shows of all time, *The Legend of Korra,* "Do the thing!" Whether you decided to create a belonging survey, lead a DEIB training, or start an apprenticeship program for underserved community members, it's time to do it.

STEP 11:
SOLICIT FEEDBACK

Once you have formed and actively launched initiatives employees can engage with, take the time to issue a short survey. It's up to you and your group members to determine what you want to measure. But remember that this is not about employees' experience at the company or demographic data so much as a way of gauging the perceived effectiveness of your work. To craft a survey people are more willing to fill out than not:

- Make anonymity the default with an option to self-disclose if folks are willing to have a deeper conversation.
- Limit the survey to seven or fewer questions.
- Keep responses multiple choice except for one or two free responses, which should be optional.

Take the surveys yourselves and make sure they take no more than five minutes to complete.

If you find you're not getting enough data through a survey, I recommend working with team leaders to see if you can do quick five-to-ten minute drop-ins on preexisting, team-specific meetings to ask employees their thoughts. The key is to try multiple approaches to get the data you need to better serve your peers.

STEP 12:
REFLECT ON OUTCOMES

Make sure to leave space for a proper retrospective when your affinity group closes out, or mostly completes, planned initiatives in the Roadmap. It's up to you whether you publish and present the results of your retrospective company-wide or keep them for internal purposes. All that matters is that you complete the cycle and make time to reflect so that you can continuously improve.

While I tailor my retrospective questions for every group I'm part of, here are the ones I find most useful across multiple situations:

1. What did we launch?
2. What succeeded? What were our biggest wins?
3. What presented challenges? What could have been done differently?
4. What is our biggest lesson learned?
5. How did we work together? What did we do that worked? How could we have worked together better?

6. How did we work with the rest of the company? What worked? What could be improved?
7. What are our highest hopes for the next initiative based on this retrospective?

Feel free to use survey results to conduct your retrospective, but don't use them alone. Your team members should be bringing their experiences, perspectives, and opinions to the table at equal weight since they are closest to the process.

COMMUNITY ENGAGEMENT

Community engagement, sometimes called service learning, is both a diversity, equity, inclusion, and belonging strategy and a retention strategy. Gen Z and Millennial employees expect their organizations will create space for them to engage civically and contribute to their communities. When this need is fulfilled, retention follows. Great Places to Work analyzed 350,000 surveys and found that people who felt their employers positively contributed to their communities were four times more likely to say their teams worked harder to get their work done, eleven times more likely to plan to stay in their organizations for the long haul, and fourteen times more likely to want to come into work each day.[12]

Surprisingly, these data points have been wildly unpopular with our client partners throughout our lifespan as a consulting firm. Most of our clients are growth-stage companies, and their leaders can't imagine sparing employee hours in this way, citing reasons like, "That volunteer work is *very* expensive in time cost," "It's up to employees to find volunteering opportunities on their own," and most common, "It feels presumptuous for us to go in and 'save' our communities, as if we know best."

Let's start with perceived time cost. If sparing a few hours of employee time on community engagement increases retention by eleven times, and attrition costs up to 50 percent of an employee's annual salary, the math works out in favor of community engagement.

The idea that employees should find their own volunteer activities is not radical. But the issue isn't that employees need workplaces uniformly to hand them volunteer opportunities; they want their jobs to be tied to something greater than their immediate workplaces. This is a natural impulse. In Marcel Mauss's groundbreaking sociological work on gift exchange, he talks about the inherent problems with workers in the new industrialized system, and notes: "The producer who carries on exchange feels once more that he is exchanging more than a product of hours of working time, but he is giving something of himself—his time, his life."[13] Employees are trading more than hours for pay at their companies, even the least engaged ones. They are giving parts of themselves to their work, including a third of their lives. They want to make that work meaningful, and no matter how mission-driven the company, it can be challenging to experience that sense of profound purpose directly in the day-to-day. Community engagement can help them see that link between what they are giving of themselves and a greater sense of impact.

Finally, the third argument around the presumptiveness and "saviorism" that can sometimes show up in community engagement. To quote a client who was "disgusted" with my suggestion that community engagement factor into his company's retention strategy, "What does a beach cleanup actually do but make a bunch of employees feel good about something that has no impact in the long term *and* reinforces the erroneous assumption that employers, rather than municipal and state governments, should be responsible for keeping our communities clean? What does my predominantly White organization do for poor Black kids on the South Side when they show up to tutor them *once?* That only helps my White employees feel good about themselves, but it does nothing for those kids." To be clear, I agree with this position. I just also think it ignores the outsized power and influence companies can have on their communities. If power were used responsibly in these situations, employees could feel that sense of impact while also genuinely helping others.

HOW TO ENGAGE WITH THE COMMUNITY RESPONSIBLY

As you determine how to bake community engagement into your organization in a way that promotes a sense of belonging and benefits community members, as always, you can develop a thoughtful proposal with a few framing questions.

Where is your community and who makes it up? What does your organization have that the community does not?

You may define your community as the area where you are headquartered, a particular subset of your customers, or the people impacted most by the work you do. It depends on what your organization does. In terms of what your organization has that the community does not: The answers may vary widely here, but a few examples are: access to capital; influence with local, state, national, or international governments; access to physical spaces; specialized knowledge; connections to networks of people, a platform, or even actual goods and services. The best community engagement initiatives are built on mutuality. The organization sees a direct tie between the community need and what they do.

When I was working in VC, my firm focused on investing in Chicago-based companies, so I defined my "community" as the Chicagoland area. I was clear on the challenges marginalized groups faced securing funding and building their businesses, so I wanted to concentrate on the part of my community where underrepresented entrepreneurs were already starting and running businesses. In partnership with local colleges, universities, community labs, and nonprofit organizations supporting entrepreneurs,

I spoke to BIPOC founders, especially those who identified as women or gender-nonconforming and asked what they needed. Obviously, they needed money. I couldn't promise as much of that as I wanted because I wasn't the one writing the checks. But when I shared that, what overwhelmingly came back was, "Thank you. I don't yet know how investing works."

In fact, many of the entrepreneurs I spoke with had limited knowledge of how raising capital worked and few in their networks who could either explain the mechanisms or make relevant recommendations. The space is *designed* to be inaccessible to give investors the upper hand. What I could give them was a full fundraising education, which they wanted—and they wanted it in their neighborhoods instead of ours. With that, I began to lead sessions all over the city, building a bank of other investors and partnering with alternative funding sources like banks and accelerators to help open up other pathways to capital. I led these programs for years, and my colleagues participated along with me. We felt the impact of helping entrepreneurs forging their own paths, even as they felt frustrated with how restrictive, exclusionary, and gatekeeping the industry was. Many of these folks went on to get funding and run successful businesses, which went a long way on our internal team, leading to a greater sense of purpose.

What does your community need (in their own words)?

To avoid "saviorism," the most important step after having defined your community is to ask them what they need. I recommend paying community members for their time, developing questions in advance, and then comparing the results from a wide enough sample to determine the right course of action. Try to interview at least ten community members. My firm generally pays $150 an interview, which ranges from thirty to ninety minutes base. The answers that come back are always surprising, useful, and insightful.

For example, in one of our nonprofit organizations, the subject of a different kind of grant-making came up. While I may have come up with a proposal for a grant-making program for a subset of the community on my own, the members themselves could tell me what grants existed already and whether they benefited from them or not, what they needed in a grant structure, and how much money was actually going to make a difference.

What level of commitment are you prepared to make?

How much time, money, and energy do you have as an organization to commit to this? Some of your employees will want to give more of their time and energy, and others less. But what is the average? Depending on this, you may consider an individual sponsorship community engagement program, where employees are given paid days off to engage civically in preapproved areas. You may decide on a more widespread effort in which the whole organization takes part. Or, something in between. Similarly, how much money do you have to dedicate? You should have a budget in mind, even if it's zero, so you can appropriately scope out your commitment.

Investment does not always have to equate to dollars allocated. Law firms routinely participate in pro bono work, where the hours themselves are the currency. I have worked with numerous consumer packaged goods companies who donate their products to communities, especially ones experiencing hunger, food insecurity, and food deserts.

How will you ensure consistency, transparency, and accountability?

The biggest mistake organizations make with community engagement is to take a "one-and-done" approach. To ensure consistency, plan for twelve months or more of activity, not just one event. Whatever kind of engagement you decide on should have a long-term bent, with a process and plan underneath it that ensures consistent support, transparency with employees and the community about the results, and accountability to meet commitments to all of the stakeholders involved.

A reporting system creates transparency and accountability. Develop a report that goes to different stakeholders. Community members should be able to see what you plan to do and receive regular updates, at least on a quarterly basis. Their voices should be part of these updates; include feedback, recommendations, and corrections. Make sure these reports create space for them to give more feedback on how things are going or what they would like to see. For employees, a more regular communication should go out letting them know when and how to engage. However, they should also receive a measures-based report quantifying the impact the organization is having through its community engagement.

Framing questions for community engagement is meant to be a start rather than an authoritative system. The main takeaway should be that there is real value to community engagement as a retention strategy and a means of supporting your broader ecosystem, but only if the stakeholders impacted are involved.

9

PROMOTION

Transform yourself to transform the world.
—GRACE LEE BOGGS

PRINCIPLE #9

*Make promotion paths transparent, information about
the process of advancement readily available, and honesty
about opportunities and employee performance—
or the lack thereof—a standard practice.*

I f we are going to talk about power in the workplace, that means
we have to talk about promotions, and specifically, who gets
them, who doesn't, and what the lucky few who do actually get
paid. This is especially important when we understand that employees dedicate more of their lives to their work than anything
else, and many expect to achieve mastery, recognition, stability,
and purpose in their careers and at their companies.

The place I experience the most hope for a representative
and equitable cohort of future leaders is the previously mentioned Women Influence Chicago (WIC) program. When the
third class was graduated, it struck me that their very existence
was radical. Sixty-two percent of the participants from that cohort identified as BIPOC. In the last two weeks of the program,

four of the participants had been promoted into senior roles, in part because it was their homework to ask.

Why was this cohort radical? Women struggle to break past the individual contributor phase of career progression. Research from PayScale shows that not only is the gender pay gap real, it persists throughout the promotion cycle. Even the women who "make it" end up making less than their man-identified counterparts. The pay gap widens as women progress in their careers, with women at the executive level making $0.69 to every dollar men make.[1] That same study showed that it also takes more time for women to progress into these leadership positions. Roughly equal percentages of men and women begin their careers as individual contributors, but by the ages thirty to forty-four, 36 percent of men became supervisors or managers while only 30 percent of women did. More strikingly, men were twice as likely to be directors or executives by age forty-five than women, and only 6 percent of women became executives at any time of their lives compared with 12 percent of men. For women of color, these numbers were even more disparate, with only 2 percent of Asian women and 2 percent of Hispanic women ever making it to the executive levels. What's notable about all of this data is that at the individual contributor levels, parity was the norm. There weren't fewer women starting at the bottom; they just never made it to the top.

It's also worth highlighting that assumptions about women based solely on perceptions of their social identity group impacts their opportunities for promotion. Societally, it is expected that women will become mothers, take on primary caretaking responsibilities, and leave their roles as a result. This mere *assumption*, according to research commissioned by Bright Horizons, leads to women incurring a wage penalty, either by being promoted more slowly or being offered lower-level and lower-paid positions, even if they never plan on having children.[2] What's more, 41 percent of employed Americans perceive working moms to be less devoted to their work and a third judged them for needing a more flexible schedule, but this same attitude was not applied to men, with some men even being paid more after having children.[3]

Given this data, it's not surprising that I am asked on a weekly basis what we are doing that is so different as to get these women from the WIC program promoted. The answer is nothing ground-breaking:

- We introduce them to each other, which shows them they are not alone in their fields, immediately leading to salary and promotion comparisons that contextualize their market value and open their eyes to what they could have somewhere else.
- We demystify the whole salary negotiation and advancement process, breaking down how companies make decisions, what benchmarks look like, and what to expect when going through the negotiation process.
- We teach them the language of negotiation, and specifically, how to flex, pivot, and adapt when they hear "No."
- We encourage them to continuously and consistently ask for promotions, instead of waiting for them. We even make it homework for some of our cohorts depending on the seasonal cycles.[4]

Granted, if women are nominated by their companies to go through this program, that means at least some of their leaders see the value in the participants, which is leverage. Yet, every time *I* bring this up, it comes across to at least some as a revelation. The messages transmitted to them by their social networks, the media, and general "business wisdom" encourage them to say "yes" to more and ask for less. Being "greedy," "grasping," "arrogant," and "self-important" are all considered deviant behaviors, ones our participants have been socialized to reject, which make them more compliant and less willing to self-advocate. And, of course, even if they do self-advocate, they are still more likely to be rejected than their man-identified colleagues.[5]

We wouldn't have to run a program like this if organizations made the promotion system transparent and clear to everyone, easily navigable, and designed to consider the social challenges marginalized groups experience getting, asking for, and fully accepting their promotions.

THE POWER OF AGENCY AND CHOICE

In leading the WIC program and also reflecting on my career experiences before becoming an entrepreneur,[6] what comes up for me isn't just the sense of unequivocal, data-backed proof that women are being denied real opportunities for advancement based on biases and assumptions, but also how big a role knowledge and language play in this phenomenon. What's missing for so many skilled, recognized, and talented underrepresented employees is an understanding of the "rules of the game."

In one of my favorite books about tech and Silicon Valley, *Uncanny Valley,* customer success manager turned tech journalist Anna Wiener explains why she couldn't succeed in her first tech job: she didn't know the expectations, the culture, or the milieu. "I didn't know that in tech, qualifications—at least the traditional ones, like advanced degrees or experience—were irrelevant when superseded by cheerful determination."[7] She was operating by a traditional understanding of how to advance in your career: pay your dues, gain experience and skills over time, and slowly but surely work your way up. But tech culture often rejects that model and replaces it with a different one that "insiders" know about, but outsiders don't.

This reminds me of what Mia Birdsong points to in *How We Show Up: Reclaiming Family, Friendship, and Community:* people from marginalized groups internalize a sense of lack of possibility. As she writes, "Part of what systemic oppression does is limit the choices and agency of the people who experience it. But it also works to convince us that we have *no* agency and *no* choice."[8]

MEASURE, MANAGE, AND RECOGNIZE PERFORMANCE

In my experience, there are two questions employees desperately want clear answers to, but often don't receive:

- How am I doing?
- How are we doing?

"How am I doing?" is the classic performance-based question. Employees want to know, measurably, tangibly, and specifically, if they are good at their jobs. Of course depending on their capacity to take critical feedback, some employees may want the answer to be "You're very good at your job, no further comments" every single time. However, I find this to be the exception rather than the rule. The challenge for many leaders is that they haven't been keeping track of performance concretely, so the answers they give are vague, incomplete, or feelings-based, which may betray biases and lead to greater confusion for employees. For this reason, even though levels and growth dimensions can sometimes create disappointment and engender eye rolls, they are vital to any healthy organization.

"How are we doing?" is a different sort of question, one tied to interpersonal relationships. The idea that people leave managers, not jobs, is related to this question. Employees want to know how they are getting along with their managers, and what they can do to have better relationships. Depending on the employee, "How are we doing?" might be part of a larger need for recognition or validation, a desire to improve the working relationship to eliminate roadblocks, or even a knee-jerk reaction to conflicts, challenges, and miscommunications.

Perhaps the best example I have of this question in practice came from an early client. The CEO of the company asked me to get involved because the friction between the vice president and the vice president's direct report was creating unease across their department. Despite the fact that the manager was performing well, and the vice president had provided the resources and information necessary for her to continue performing well, they were barely on speaking terms. So, I interviewed them individually to get a sense of where the conflict was coming from and then called them into a mediation. I started by having each describe examples of times when the other had let them down or not kept a promise (themes from their individual interviews). Then I asked the other person to respond with their recollection of the events. Normally, this approach worked because the underlying issue was a failure to understand the other person's perspective. But in this case they already agreed on each other's perspectives. The energy in the room felt heavy and fraught. Finally, I just blurted out to the vice president: "Why do you *like* her?" Taken aback, the vice president rattled off a list of reasons, all genuine and detailed. The manager immediately burst into tears. After composing herself, she said, "I didn't know you liked me. I always felt you didn't." This led to the vice president sharing he had imagined *she* didn't like *him,* so he avoided her. I prompted them to share why they liked each other. By the end of the session, they had actually reconciled, and their relationship noticeably improved over the next few months.

Because of the emotional and social nature of the "How are we doing?" question, I find my clients are more willing to engage in addressing "How am I doing?" The trick is that satisfying, productive answers to the latter question require a baseline of shared understanding and open communication between managers and employees.

Social identity can impact that sense of open communication. As inclusion strategist Vernā Myers points out, "Sloppy sentimentalism happens when a manager finds it hard to give constructive feedback to a supervisee from a one-down group or hold the supervisee accountable for his or her behavior. Out of a sense of superiority, someone from a one-up group may decide what is best for someone from a one-down group without asking what the person needs and wants."[9] This is a dangerous way to measure performance and give feedback because it means that a manager's assumptions about a person's social identity inform what opportunities they receive, including the opportunity to learn and grow from their mistakes. In some ways, I think the "How am I doing?" and "How are we doing?" questions map, respectively, to equality and equity. First, we need to develop a system that minimizes the chances of sloppy sentimentalism because it's repeatable, automatic, and uniformly applied. Then, we need to make sure managers are equipped to have frank, transparent conversations with each of their employees about that system and how they are collaborating.

"HOW AM I DOING?" AND THE VALUE OF LEVELS AND GROWTH DIMENSIONS

Levels are tied to one of the greater goals of an organization, and they provide a platform for individual career growth across the organization. At their core, levels ensure individuals know where they are today, how they can move in the organization, and what it will take to develop in their careers. Levels also ensure that people in the same roles end up with comparable responsibilities and are measured the same way for them. In other words, they are maps that clearly define responsibilities and required levels of competency and skill based on a person's role in the organization. If used correctly, they let people know what is expected of them, and they help guide conversations around performance.

As many of my clients have pointed out, levels can feel dissatisfying to their employees. Sometimes, employees disagree with where their managers and leaders place them, believing their contributions are greater than their current level. Other times, employees excel in their level, and in a perfect system *would* advance, but company needs, budget constraints, or structural challenges mean they end up stuck. While levels are an imperfect system, these issues aren't solved when they are eliminated; instead, ambiguity reigns. If an employee believes they are doing a better job than their manager thinks they are, that fact will remain; there just won't be concrete behaviors and criteria to refer to when the disagreement comes to a head. Similarly, if the organization doesn't have room for another leader, whether you have a levels system or not, there won't be a path forward for that exceptional employee. The difference is that with levels, that conversation will likely happen sooner and with greater clarity.

Now, it's definitely possible that employee pushback on levels can come down to flaws in their architecture, which is why I suggest developing a flexible structure for them that can be revised and revisited regularly. When I work with organizations to design their levels systems, I usually apply a few principles.

ADVANCEMENT TRACKS

Levels should be developed for both individual contributor and people management tracks. In many organizations the only way to grow is to manage others; but plenty of folks either don't like managing or have technical skills so valuable that to take them away from that work creates gaps. So, as you set the levels for your organization, make sure to chart out what advancement looks like in both tracks. Having simple definitions for individual contributors and people managers helps:

- *Individual contributors* are experts in their domains who are measured on their work products and outputs. They may be teachers and team supporters, but they are not expected to manage others.
- *People managers* are focused on giving their reports the direction, coaching, support, and growth opportunities they need to produce better work products and outputs. They are measured not on their deliverables but on how well their direct reports perform. They may contribute to projects and produce their own individual work products, but their primary expectation is to manage others.

GROWTH DIMENSIONS

Growth dimensions are groups of skills, behaviors, and knowledge areas that reflect the performance standard of working at an organization. Growth dimensions encompass both competencies and values, and they map to individual contributor and management tracks. What makes them so necessary for levels is that they define not only the outcomes expected of employees, but also how they are expected to reach those outcomes. At Ethos, we have a few growth dimensions that apply to each employee and are generally defined.

GROWTH DIMENSION	DETAILS
Bias for Action	• Demonstrates an ability to bring ideas and strategies to life professionally and creatively • Is quick to take responsibility • Independently jumps in to solve problems

GROWTH DIMENSION	DETAILS
Quality	• Prioritizes work to meet the needs of clients, colleagues, and the community • Understands big picture goals and incorporates them into work • Pays close attention to the details • Engages in consistent, dedicated practice
Strategic Thinking	• Knows the "why" behind everything they do • Shows an orientation toward being strategic and purpose-driven • Believes in possibility and the potential for future growth • Sees every challenge, obstacle, and experience as an opportunity
Learning Orientation	• Continuously seeks new information • Brings new research and ideas into the company • Is more interested in learning than winning
Emotional Intelligence	• Goes out of their way to listen to and understand others • Effectively identifies and regulates their own emotions • Understands the emotions of others • Adapts to changing contexts to manage relationships
Effective Communication	• Communicates clearly, openly, and with radical candor • Articulates needs, problems, and opportunities in a way that helps others understand • Exhibits digital soft skills • Engages in regular feedback practices

The expectations for these general growth dimensions and how they are applied may change or become more specific as they are matched with levels across departments. Similarly, while these are Ethos levels, your organization may need to consider different growth dimensions; the process of developing growth dimensions must take place in conjunction with understanding the needs and goals of the larger organization.

DESCRIBING LEVELS

The most challenging part of developing levels is describing them. Generally, I create a "Master Levels Framework" that abstracts basic responsibilities and expectations at any level, and then I work with department leaders to take the master and customize it for their teams.

Within departments, there are three main components per level: title, role description, and growth dimensions. Each is defined and determined by the people managers in a given department. The title and actual level number, as well as the growth dimensions, inform compensation.

To advance from one level to another, team members must exhibit competence in all of their assigned growth dimensions and begin performing at the next level. Competence here means consistently and appropriately demonstrating that growth dimension.

Somewhere in your Levels Philosophy or other framing document defining the levels structure, it's important to define how these levels work in practice. Two ideas that I often highlight in mine are:

- People managers will work with their direct reports to share what is required of them in performing at the next level above; this is determined based on the team's emerging needs. Team members pursuing promotions from one level to another will be asked to take on additional responsibilities that are a level above where they are today. This ensures that they can quickly step into the new roles upon promotion.
- Based on the needs of the team, there won't always be a clear opportunity for immediate advancement to management. Regardless of whether or not there are opportunities, people managers will clearly communicate the expectations for advancement to their team members.

NUMBER OF LEVELS

I worked with an organization with a startling 112 levels. While the system was as detailed as humanly possible, it was almost impossible to navigate, and employees constantly lost sight of where they were and where they were going. Plus, having so many levels when an organization is growing ends up rigidly boxing them in when they aren't yet certain about all the products, programs, or services they will produce, let alone which roles will be responsible for them. I generally like to start with no more than five to seven levels in an organization, with the first level representing entry level positions, and the last one to two levels representing the senior leadership positions.

Levels should be tied to different performance expectations depending on proficiency required by a given role. As a general rule, I structure the number of levels around three categories: entry, mid, and senior.

ENTRY	MID	SENIOR
Team members are given both the problem and the solution, and they are expected to follow the appropriate steps in order to drive the necessary outcomes.	Team members are given the problem and expected to find their solution on their own. They may require support from entry roles to realize the solution and senior roles to better define the problem and think about how to approach it in new and different ways.	Team members find both the problem and the solution. They may enlist others to help inform and realize both; however, they are expected to be able to determine who should be involved and why based on their complete understanding of the full work process.

In some cases, entry or mid-level team members may be able to find both the problem and the solution on a given project. This doesn't mean they automatically belong at the senior level. This model is based on mastery. Does the team member *almost always* find both the problem and solution? Do they do this competently and reliably? This is how we determine their level.

STEPS

To ensure we're allowing for enough adaptability and flexibility within roles, as well as recognizing high performance that doesn't necessarily equate to performing at a level above the current role, I recommend creating "Steps" that can be added into the levels framework. Steps represent a move within a level and may result in a pay increase without a title change.

I usually give myself the option to add up to three steps per level. For ease of understanding, I will label these steps A, B, and C:

- Step A is where everyone starts at a given level. They are doing the work, but still learning the ropes and developing their domain expertise and role acumen.
- Step B indicates that a team member has mastered that level and is meeting all expectations within their range of responsibilities.
- Step C means that the team member has mastered their current level and has begun performing a few of the responsibilities at the next level without demonstrating full competency in that role.

THE POWER OF POSITIVE FEEDBACK

We all have an innate need to feel "special" and part of the group. When we do diversity, equity, inclusion, and belonging surveys at Ethos, we usually find our clients score low on questions around recognition and positive feedback. In particular, we find that in response to the question "The right people are rewarded and recognized," employees from self-identified marginalized groups answer "Disagree" or "Strongly Disagree" two to three times more often than ones in self-identified dominant groups.

Healthy relationships aren't just characterized by how people stick with one another through bad times, but how much they celebrate good ones. Employees need to feel appreciated and celebrated in order to feel belonging.

To make sure you treat feedback as a vehicle for praise instead of focusing only on critiques, take a few steps on a regular basis.

1. *Be generous with praise.* When it comes up for you, don't keep it to yourself, but share it openly and liberally.

2. *Make sure people feel seen and recognized for what matters to them.* This means understanding what they value in themselves and in their work and recognizing them when they meet those values.

3. *Encourage others around you to be generous with praise.* Give shoutouts to people who give shoutouts. Build a "shoutouts" channel into your digital communication platform. Remind people in meetings to celebrate their peers.

4. *Trade in generic "good jobs" for specific, sincere, and personal feedback.* It may take longer, but it'll be more memorable to folks because it's tied to examples. You don't have to give a speech every time; just let folks know why it was a good job.

5. *Don't be afraid to celebrate when things go right.* Sometimes it seems as if my clients are waiting for the other shoe to drop, and that by saying something went well, they are inviting catastrophe. This superstitious caution denies folks the chance to feel proud of what they did, which will help create the momentum and resilience to withstand the bad things that might come up in the future.

"HOW ARE WE DOING?" AND THE POWER OF FEEDBACK

In theory, once you have levels in place, performance reviews should be easy to manage. You now have a path employees can move along and clear criteria you can use to measure performance. And yet, for many of the clients I work with, the challenges have just begun.

One of my favorite stories about the danger of being "too nice" in giving feedback comes from a conversation with a Chief People Officer at a tech company in Chicago. At 500 employees and millions in profits, they had progressed past the startup phase and moved into "established." They had clear levels, growth plans, performance measurement practices and systems, and standard training for anyone in a leadership role. But these structures weren't enough to minimize performance-based confusion and miscommunication.

The Chief People Officer met with one of the recruiters from the underperforming team. Carefully and compassionately, she laid out a history of their underperformance, and the reasons they would be entering a six-week Performance Improvement Plan. If they did not improve, they would be terminated at the end of that six-week period. Two weeks later, this same person asked to schedule a meeting about the open Director of Recruiting position. In that short meeting, the underperforming recruiter made a case for how they ought to be considered for the role. Gently, the Chief People Officer said, "But, you have to understand, we can't consider you for this position when you're on a Performance Improvement Plan." To which the recruiter replied, "What?" This was news to them. In a post-mortem of this situation, I realized that not once in the conversation had the Chief People Officer ever said the words "Performance Improvement Plan" or termination. The recruiter, who had what I called "happy ears," heard the six-week ultimatum as encouragement from their boss's boss to really push themselves to level up.

Levels are the structure. They provide clarity when properly applied. And feedback is their delivery mechanism. The answer to "How are we doing?" is determined largely on whether employees get the information they need and how they get it. Specifically, if you feel you have a healthy rapport with your direct report and can talk candidly and openly, you're more likely to be honest with them. But everyone, and I mean everyone, has employees who are hard to read or hard to manage, and the idea of giving them constructive feedback is blood-curdling. I have managed employees I am legitimately afraid of because they lash out when threatened, because I know they are quick to cry, or because I feel guilty about giving constructive feedback to someone I like and want to like me back. What has saved me from avoiding conflict and just saying nothing has been structure. And when it comes to feedback, there are three types of structures that help keep me honest and brave in talking about employee performance: performance reviews, feedback in one-on-ones, and ad hoc feedback.

Performance Reviews get a bad rap. At least once a year, I see a think piece about how performance reviews don't work and why we should abolish them. Reasons include: they take too long to do and therefore are incomplete and poorly done; bias hurts employees from marginalized groups; no one takes them seriously; and people don't give feedback because they are waiting for the review season. Yet I often find myself reinstituting a performance-review process in organizations that eliminated them. Why?

Because when done well, performance reviews hold both sides accountable to "How am I doing?" and "How are we doing?" The formality and time-boxed nature of performance reviews often mean both sides are *more* willing to engage in real dialogue about what's happening at work than they would be on a day-to-day basis. (But we will get to day-to-day feedback soon.)

So, let's address these antiperformance review arguments one by one:

- *They take too long to do and therefore are incomplete and poorly done.* My first response to this argument is: Why? Is the process overly complex or unclearly defined? Do people managers have too many direct reports? Do direct reports have too many competing responsibilities? Or do they just not see the value? Here's where I think a focus group or research interviews could benefit—let's figure out the root cause of the timing issue, as well as what people need to get out of these reviews. Generally, in our client organizations, the solution to this problem isn't getting rid of performance reviews but simplifying the process and establishing its value on all sides.
- *Bias hurts employees from marginalized groups.* I take the bias argument very seriously. And, I don't think eliminating reviews altogether actually helps with this problem. As we have established, research shows that women and BIPOC get less frequent and lower-quality feedback than those in the dominant groups.[10] When people don't receive feedback, they are less likely to know their worth in negotiations, are ill equipped to assess their strengths and weaknesses, and are less able to build the confidence they need to proactively seek promotions or make risky decisions. Another option is to name the kinds of bias that enter the process, train people managers on what they are and how to avoid them, and run practice sessions. Also, performance reviews shouldn't be the *only* feedback mechanism; employees should have these on top of feedback in one-on-ones and in their work.
- *No one takes performance reviews seriously.* Again, we have to probe into why. Is it because of one of the other reasons on this list? Does the culture avoid honest feedback, making these meetings light on content? Are they an afterthought? Is accountability not part of the

organization's values or practices? At this point, we have to establish why we want to give feedback, including what kinds. From there, the mechanisms can be matched to purpose, and regularly communicated to everyone involved.

- *People don't give feedback because they are waiting for the review season.* This is an excuse made by people who don't want to give feedback. Eliminating performance reviews provides them a legitimate reason to give less feedback. I coach folks who have this fear, and we can usually break through it by understanding what they are afraid of and where they have knowledge gaps.

With all this in mind, I have a few practices I institute in performance reviews that help me lead positive, effective, and illuminating meetings:

- *Compensation and performance discussions are separate.* The stakes are too high around compensation to have an honest discussion around performance without it. If I am combining these discussions, as a manager, my view of my budget affects how I rate my employees. If I don't have a big budget, I am more likely to unconsciously say they aren't doing as well; if I have a surplus, I might tell them they are performing better than they are because I know I have money to spend. Separately, employees worrying about how to negotiate well won't actually take the time to reflect on what they need to improve their performance. Setting up prescheduled compensation conversations outside of review season helps address this dual challenge.
- *Stick to your growth dimensions.* The whole point of a structure like growth dimensions is to establish consistency. Measure prospective candidates and

current employees according to the same criteria, track all of your feedback for current employees on a scorecard you both can view over time, and make sure that you are focusing on behaviors tied to the ones outlined. If you need to change your growth dimensions because new situations emerge (and they will), make a case for why, and let your team know before you ever get into a review.

- *Prepare in advance.* To be thoughtful and honest, you have to consider this person's performance holistically, as well as your own as their manager. This means blocking off time before the day of the review to look at those growth dimensions and reflect on where your employee is.

- *Nothing in the review should be a surprise.* Performance reviews are not the be all and end all. They're a dedicated time to reflect deeply together, which in today's overcommitted, task-switching work environment is rare and necessary. But there should never be a situation where someone is hearing for the first time that they are underperforming or that they are really good at what they do. If you find yourself bringing up new information, this must be acknowledged, and you must take responsibility for helping the employee understand, and if applicable, improve in these areas.

- *Top-down feedback isn't enough.* My direct reports lead their reviews. They start by telling me how the last quarter has been (because we do quarterly reviews), and they self-evaluate how they are doing, as well as let me know how I am doing. Our review is a conversation about our performance on both sides. Since my team is relatively small, we have not yet instituted 360° feedback, but I am a big advocate for this practice. Peers often have a better sense of their colleagues' performance because they are closer to their actual work.

- *Check your biases.* Literally. Remember that bias table in the Recruiting chapter? When I go through my performance reviews, I have that table open in front of me, and I check everything I have written on my review scorecard ahead of time to make sure I am not falling into one of those biases.

Feedback in one-on-ones helps establish the habit and make the act of giving and receiving feedback automatic and recurring. For this reason, in all one-on-one agendas, I recommend a feedback section. This might be a category called "Improvement," with four questions participants have to answer in their weekly sessions:[11]

1. What is one way we as an organization can improve this week?
2. What is one thing I am currently doing that is effective?
3. What is one thing I can do more of to be effective?
4. What is one thing I can do less of to be effective?

We take turns answering these questions, and the results are usually informative. Framing the feedback in terms of improving the organization's performance helps depersonalize some of the feedback while focusing on what's working already. When I present this, however, the most commonly asked question I receive is: "What do I do about sensitive employees who take feedback personally?"

First, if an employee takes feedback so personally as to deter folks from giving it, this is a performance issue, and they will have to receive feedback on their ability to take feedback. Meta-ness aside, I believe in the power of what Melissa Dahl, author of *Cringeworthy: A Theory of Awkwardness*, calls being an anthropologist, trying to understand rather than convince. Why are they taking this feedback personally?

When people can't understand others, it's often because they feel misunderstood themselves, so it stands to reason that starting from a place of empathy can help them see where you are coming from. For me, coming from a place of understanding means going back to an important lesson from the founder of neuroleadership coaching, David Rock. In *Your Brain at Work*, he highlights that "Exclusion and rejection is physiologically painful. A feeling of being less than activates the same brain regions as physical pain." When constructive feedback feels like rejection, it is literally painful, and the person who reacts to it with sensitivity is merely experiencing a human response to pain.

One way to make the feedback less painful is to give it in a framework Rock terms "ARIA," an acronym for "Awareness, Reflection, Insight, Action." I use his framework to set up difficult conversations around performance like this:

- *Awareness:* Present an example of what behavior needs to change. Ask the person to distill the problem or root cause down into one sentence.
- *Reflection:* Help them reflect on how they are thinking about solving the problem as opposed to the solution. This activates the right hemisphere in your brain by conjuring high-level thought. It's through this process that the brain starts making new connections.
- *Insight:* In this stage, a group of neurons fire in unison, releasing energy and an insight with it. You'll notice an "aha" moment.
- *Action:* Once they have the insight, help them take steps to translate it into action. This is where you can go into a traditional feedback framework.

Ad hoc feedback can be key because you won't always have a performance review or a one-on-one to give feedback, and there might be a temptation to avoid feedback unless there's a meeting on the calendar. I say this coming from my own experience; I often find myself filing away a specific incident or situation until the next time we meet formally. This, however, breaks my general guideline of making sure feedback isn't a surprise. And, it's going to be less of a surprise if it's delivered closer to when something happened. Plus, I find that it's easier to forget to give positive feedback than constructive feedback, which skews employees' self-perception and throws away an excellent opportunity to show them what good work looks like in concrete rather than abstract terms.

But giving feedback is uncomfortable! It's an awkward conversation, especially depending on the type of the relationship you have with the other person. That's where structure comes into play. Having a framework to put feedback through makes the process easier. For this reason, I love Situation-Behavior-Impact (see Figure 7).

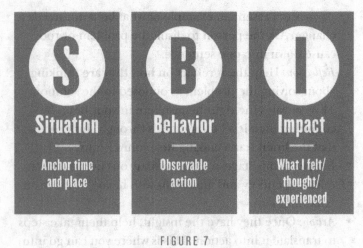

S	B	I
Situation	Behavior	Impact
Anchor time and place	Observable action	What I felt/ thought/ experienced

FIGURE 7

Whenever the need to give feedback strikes—again, whether negative or positive—deliver it according to this mechanism. Here are two examples of Situation-Behavior-Impact in practice:

POSITIVE (Delivered in a Slack channel for positive feedback): *Shoutout to Lexi for exemplifying our value of Start with Why. Lexi is committed to listening and empathizing. This morning I went to her with a problem that came up over the holiday and she was open to talking through a solution with me (situation). Lexi listens intently and asks questions (behavior) about what I share with her, and I've never felt judged when I talk through my mistakes or challenges. Thank you for helping me solve my problem this morning (impact) and thank you for being a big part of why I love being a manager (impact).*

CONSTRUCTIVE (Delivered in a 1:1): *When we came together for our team offsite to decide on our quarterly strategy (situation), every time I offered a new milestone idea, you emphasized that we didn't have enough information, should hold on moving forward, and should change the subject (behavior). When your team member suggested it would be fine to make a "good" decision instead of a "perfect one," you responded by saying they didn't have enough context to make suggestions and really needed to table the issue (behavior). This slowed down our decision-making process on milestones and made others in the room hesitant to share their milestones (impact) for fear they wouldn't be heard.*

Both of these were delivered within a few hours of the situation, and both were well received. They took no more than thirty seconds to give, and no one had to interpret what I was thinking. This, of course, is the greatest benefit of feedback: it makes the implicit explicit.

AVOIDING BIASED FEEDBACK

With all of these feedback tools established, it's worth exploring the flip side of this phenomenon: biased feedback. The fear of delivering bigoted, discriminatory, or offensive feedback keeps many managers from telling employees what they need to hear, and that lurking fear comes from a real place. People from marginalized groups often have plenty of examples of microaggressive and oppressive feedback they have received from managers.

So, how do you eliminate bias from the feedback process without eliminating feedback altogether?

The first step is familiarizing yourself with what that bias would look like in action. Take, for example, Figure 8, originally published in a *Harvard Business Review* analysis of language from 81,000 performance reviews.[12]

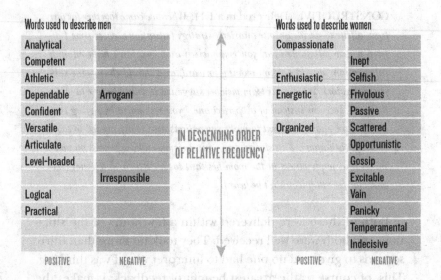

FIGURE 8

"Frivolous," "vain," "gossip," and "temperamental" stand out as gendered terms used to describe women at some point in their careers. One of the clear divides between how men and women were described in their reviews is that while men were more often described in terms of being logical and analytical, women were described in emotional terms, whether they were good or bad. This is a long-standing stereotype that contributes to the wage gap and also the phenomenon of women being pushed into to support roles rather than operational ones.[13]

As you are putting together your feedback, reflect on common biases and stereotypes. Review your microaggressions table while you're at it. Most of all, make sure you have the job description and any notes you have about specific projects the person worked on in front of you. I've created a decision tree to help you through this work.

The decision tree can be found at http://www.alidamirandawolff .com/bookreaders.

PROMOTING EQUITABLY AND INCLUSIVELY

Even with a levels system, performance reviews process, and managers trained in the art of giving and receiving feedback, promoting equitably and inclusively is still far from an easy process. For one, there's hidden discrimination to contend with; namely, the tendency to help those who are like you more than those who are not.

The example that comes to mind of this phenomenon in practice is of the injured quilter. The quilter in question, Carla Kaplan, had a kitchen accident that sent her to the emergency room with a badly bleeding hand. The injury was serious enough that she went to the Yale New Haven Hospital emergency room where she asked the doctor to save her hand because she was a quilter. He proceeded to work on her hand competently until a student spotted her and identified her as a Yale professor. The ER doctor, upon realizing her status, brought in the best hand surgeon in New England. His bias toward a fellow Yale employee meant she went from getting good treatment to the best treatment.[14]

This tendency to privilege some over others finds its way into the promotions process, meaning that to create the conditions for people to feel valued and needed, those who have the power to promote must show vigilance in tracking who gets what opportunities. This means tracking across your organization how people are moving along your levels, and tracking the percentages based on social identity categories relative to representation in the company *and* in terms of your local and national populations. If, for example, your company's city is 24 percent Black, your employee base is 12 percent Black, and only 2 percent of all promotions awarded are to Black people, you know something is happening. You may not know exactly what that something is, but the numbers create a concrete benchmark to check yourself against.

I recently met a lot of resistance to this process by one of our client organizations in the managed IT services space. The issue came not from tracking the numbers, but my insistence that these numbers should be transparently shared with the organization as another form of accountability to change. The block came up like this: "There's a lot of diversity in our organization, but we don't retain it, and the numbers show that we also don't promote it. Won't that disillusion our employees?" My reply was straightforward: "Don't you think everyone can see this happening? They notice when their colleagues leave; they also notice who their leaders are."

Tracking data doesn't usually create tensions that didn't exist before; it brings these tensions to light. Employees at this company, based on our anonymous surveys, already knew the "diversity problem" in the organization was tied to advancement. However, they tended to think it was greater than the raw numbers revealed because they were interpreting what was happening instead of seeing it directly mapped out.

Apart from keeping clear metrics around advancement in place and sharing them with the organization's employees, there are four practices that help create environments that support equitable and inclusive growth:

1. *Equal Pay for Equal Work:* I am the first to admit that I haven't found an ideal solution to the equitable pay issue. I have tried tiered compensation built around individual employee need (too subjective and hard to measure) and including reparations in pay (complicated and often too narrowly focused on one group, as opposed to the many who have suffered under patriarchal and racist systems). What I have found that works is creating pay bands that promote equal pay for equal work, as well as an annual wage audit process where all salaries are compared, evaluated, and corrected.

2. *Negotiations Process:* Given the fraught nature of negotiations, and the ways in which only some stand to gain from them, I sometimes recommend eliminating negotiations altogether. For example, at Ethos, we have a "no negotiations on pay" policy designed for equality-based reasons. We engage in open accounting and open salaries, which means everyone knows what everyone else makes. We also calculate the maximum amount we can afford in pay and still stay solvent before offering prospective candidates and advancing employees their compensation packages. Because we practice equal pay for equal work, negotiations often create unnecessary divisions and inequalities, especially because we often can't afford to adjust everyone at that level's salary. With that said, we are a very small organization. Negotiations can and do make sense in other places. But if you're going to allow negotiations, think about equity. Which folks are least likely to negotiate? Why? Everyone in your company, and I mean absolutely everyone, should know your stance on when, how, and with whom to initiate negotiations.[15]

3. *Sponsorship:* Sponsors and mentors are not the same thing, but organizations often treat them as if they are. Mentors guide and share experiences to help employees navigate their careers. Sponsors may also engage in this kind of guidance, but they primarily focus on supporting their charges in navigating office politics, breaking down what it takes to succeed inside their companies, and advocating for their sponsees. Companies encouraging sponsorship and creating sponsorship programs shift the impetus from the employee who must confront the odds to succeed, to the company, which can create the relationships and the access to make success possible.

4. *Succession Planning:* Succession planning is fundamentally different from leveling because it considers what to do in the case that leaders retire or leave the organization. It's actually a business best practice because it mitigates risk, promotes growth, and limits the possibility of failing due to power vacuums or outside intervention. Still, according to the National Association of Corporate Directors, fewer than one in four private company boards say they have a formal succession plan in place.[16] The other advantage of succession planning is that it allows for the organization to thoughtfully and concertedly consider how to make space for and invest in employees of marginalized groups so they may fill the positions as they open. Instead of grooming the people we like for success, we can look at the whole slate of employees within the organization and prepare them for leadership, tailoring our investments to the individual needs of the folks we want to eventually take over.

SUCCESSFUL DIVERSE TEAMS[17]

What often goes unsaid in workplaces is how well employees perform (which in a perfect system determines how they advance) is dependent on their social environments. However, if the social environment is dysfunctional, out of sync, or toxic, that creates significant barriers and hurdles to improvement and promotion.[18]

Early on in my diversity management program, we were discussing the power of diverse teams. Naturally, we were all listing the benefits of diversity in our own organizations. That's when our facilitator, Sukari Pinnock Fitts, said, "The thing about diverse teams is that they aren't more successful; they actually underperform. Unless they engage in team development. Then they outperform non-diverse teams."

Her central argument was simple. When we are different from one another, we are more likely to have opposing points of view, which leads to conflict. Without appropriately establishing norms and boundaries, getting to know each other, and setting mutual goals, team members may find themselves coming into conflict so much they can't move together toward high performance. This argument highlights our collective cultural (see: American) fear of conflict. We shy away from people who are unlike us because we fear clashing with them, even when so much of the business thought leadership today emphasizes that healthy conflict drives more innovation and better results.

As someone who not only works on a diverse team but also facilitates change in both homogenous and diverse teams, I started investigating how conflict specifically manifests on diverse teams, which ultimately led me to apply conflict management principles and models in several different company systems.

What I found is that humans evolved with "toward" and "away" responses. We move toward those who are like us (friends) and away from those who are different (perceived foes). We are so primed to associate with one another based on the similarity that even the smallest shared social identification brings us together and amplifies the likelihood of intergroup bias. In other words, the "us and them" impulse is strong.

There are a number of early childhood studies that show this dynamic at play. For example, a 2011 study found that five-year-olds randomly grouped with other unfamiliar children by color (red or blue) preferred pictures of children wearing the color that corresponded to their own groups.[19] As *Mapping Innovation* author Greg Satell points out, these preferences manifest in adults, too. In a study of adults randomly assigned as "leopards" or "tigers," fMRI studies noted intergroup bias and hostility toward the other group, regardless of race.[20] Bias requires both a sense of similarity and of difference. The perceived difference may breed hostility and conflict.

Despite these findings, diverse teams are not destined to underperform unless they can find common ground. There is a body of evidence showing that homogenous teams underperform precisely because they experience more "comfortable" environments, while diverse teams overperform due to the increased effort necessary to work within them.

As David Rock, Heidi Grant, and Jacqui Grey emphasize in their 2016 analysis for the *Harvard Business Review*, homogeneous teams collaborate easily, understand each other inherently, and are prone to make the wrong judgments.[21]

For example, in a 2009 study published in *Personality and Social Psychology Bulletin*, fraternity and sorority members who are more likely to self-select into groups based on similarity and a strong sense of shared group identity engaged in an experiment to solve a murder mystery.[22] Teams either remained homogeneous throughout the experiment or introduced "outsiders." Homogenous teams reported feeling like they were progressing more smoothly and collaborating more effectively, while the diverse teams found the experience harder, and the participants felt less confident in their final decisions. Yet the homogenous teams made the wrong judgments, getting the answer right only 29 percent of the time. Groups with outsiders arrived at the correct solution 60 percent of the time. The work felt harder and the outcomes were more likely to be successful.

We are more fearful of outsiders and tend to find collaboration harder with them at the very same time that we produce better work through that partnership. The conflict we experience in more diverse teams is precisely why we see better results on them. We just have to make sure that conflict isn't so explosive that collaboration stalls completely.

When it comes to conflict, I have an almost pathological need to make everyone happy, and I will neglect my own needs or pursue the wrong path if I imagine it will make others feel better. On a diverse team, this means that I personally feel wiped out during collaborations and can shy away from the conflict necessary to get us to the best final product. And I'm a DEIB practitioner. Consequently, I've had to learn behavioral modifications that allow for me to be fully present with conflict and manage it so that I can engage with it healthily. I can't pretend to be 100 percent perfect in this practice, but I can say that I've made noticeable progress with the following four principles I've come up with for managing (not eliminating) conflict on teams:

1. *Conflict management is about looking for a mutual goal.* At the beginning of team development, we all align on one goal we can get behind. Our thinking, strategies, processes, and practices may all be different and divergent after that point, but we will have an anchor to ground us and remind us of the value of fully engaging with each other in collaboration.

2. *Healthy conflicts involve parties who respond rather than react.* Emotional regulation is essential to healthy conflict. That means creating enough mental space for

oneself to assess a situation and intentionally mobilize energy before engaging.

3. *Conflicts end with a decision.* This means clearly stating what is going to happen, even if it's "agree to disagree." Whether the decision is not to change at all or to pursue a whole new path, it must be explicitly stated and recognized in the group.

4. *The conversation doesn't end with the conflict resolution.* Once conflict on a team is resolved, I have observed a tendency (including my own) to avoid team members for fear that somehow the conflict will start over. However, this approach allows for the conflict to reopen, especially based on a feeling that "We aren't talking so something must be wrong." Bonding after strain and struggle leads to a deeper connection.

The idea of responding rather than reacting often feels out of reach for many of the teams I coach and facilitate.

That's why I highly recommend the Above the Line/Below the Line exercise (see Figure 9). I adapted the tool from the Conscious Leadership model and through watching the facilitator and innovation coach Lori Lovens lead a version of this in one of her seminars.

Breaking this model down, if you're above the line, you're coming from a place of openness, curiosity, and commitment to learning. If you're below it, you're defensive, closed off, and committed to being right. It's natural to vacillate between the two throughout a single conversation. The key is to notice when the change happens and take a step back. When conflict starts to feel out of hand, and you notice yourself getting heated, simply take a pause and ask yourself:

1. Am I "above the line" or "below the line"?
2. What is being threatened here?

Staying "Above the Line"

Curious
Open
Committed to learning

(Love)

_____

(Fear)

Defensive/Defended
Closed
Committed to being right

FIGURE 9

3. What am I thinking that this conversation says about me?
4. Has my top priority shifted to preserving my ego?

By the time you have finished this sequence, most likely you will be above your feelings instead of inside them, giving you the mental space to recalibrate and focus on the content of what is being shared, rather than the more fraught context. In the beginning, the tool can feel clunky; the first few times I used it, I would excuse myself to refill my teacup and work through the questions on the trip to the kettle and back. Now, this happens for me in a span of about six seconds because it's become such an ingrained habit.[23]

We shouldn't be afraid of the conflict that might arise from coming up against another culture or social identity–shaped worldview. Instead, we should look for the opportunity to learn something that helps us better understand our world and engage with it differently.

PROTECTION

―――――――― PRINCIPLE #10 ――――――――

Safety is our most basic human need; belonging,
self-actualization, or any higher orders of needs
cannot exist unless people feel safe first.

D uring much of 2020, I was coming to terms with the fact that after thirteen years of navigating the healthcare system, having multiple surgeries, and going through treatment after treatment, I could count myself as a member of the invisible disability community. Chronic illness was and is a part of my daily life, and internalized shame around disability led me to make decisions that further compromised my health. During this journey, I realized that in all my work to understand social identity, I had avoided disability as a focus area because of my own personal feelings. This seemed like a major gap, especially considering one out of four people in the US has a disability. I sought to correct that gap by forming relationships with community organizations, speaking openly about my own experiences with chronic illness, and reaching out to fellow DEIB practitioners and disability consultants to help me and the members of my firm better understand how to advocate for employees with disabilities in our client organizations. What this experience did for me was threefold: it reminded me that no one is the expert on all these issues, the work of DEIB involves constant self-education, and this work is not meant to be done alone.

When I first started hiring folks at Ethos, people asked me why I didn't just go it alone and cut out all the responsibilities that come with managing a team and running a business. I used to say it was because with more people, we could actually scale belonging in organizations instead of being limited by my capacity to do the work. I still think that is true, and I now also understand that one person simply can't know enough about all of the facets of social identity. A coalition of people is more successful than just one person in disentangling oppressive power structures and creating "fair shots."

For this reason, I suggest that developing the policies, processes, and practices that protect employees from harm, discrimination, harassment, bullying, and misconduct should be an interactive process. The employees you want to keep safe have to be involved in defining their experiences and what safety means for them. While this chapter focuses on the specific actions I have taken with the support of my own community of practitioners and groups of employees, more than any other chapter, it's meant to be taken as a blueprint. It is for you to construct, maintain, and repair the structures you build off this plan in collaboration with the people you serve.

POLICIES

What does it mean to keep employees safe? What can we reasonably expect organizations to do when it comes to safety? And what does it mean to be held accountable for the actions of others?

These are perhaps the thorniest questions leaders are facing today, and ideologically speaking, I haven't found a consensus on any of them. What I have found, though, is a starting point.

That starting point is the act of reviewing, redrafting, and developing the policies that serve as guides for how to keep people safe with the explicit lenses of antiracism, antisexism, antiableism, antiheterosexism, and antixenophobia.[1] By considering social identity in creating something people can concretely learn, engage with, and follow, you begin laying the groundwork for safe environments.

Before I dive into how, it's worth calling out that overemphasizing policy above all else can harm employees in marginalized groups. In the Centre for Community Organizations (COCo) guide to white supremacy in organizations, the authors delve into the specific characteristics of white supremacy culture that cause damage interpersonally and structurally to BIPOC.[2] In their analysis of "perfectionism," they call out "worship of the written word" as a characteristic of white supremacy cultures, especially because it is overvalued as a form of communication to the exclusion of other modes, privileges those with writing skills even in organizations where person-to-person interactions are key to the mission, dismisses different learning and processing styles, undervalues emotion, and holds BIPOC to different standards than White people.[3] In the latter case, they cite how dress codes might be stringently applied to BIPOC but loosely interpreted and enforced with White employees.

This is not to say *don't write your policies down*. COCo acknowledges that not writing things down is often a strategy of organizations looking to consolidate and hold on to power at the expense of their employees, and that not having clear policies and information about them widens disparities and leads to the continuation of problematic patterns. Instead, it's a reminder to enlist others in making your policies accessible to different processing styles. Document them and share them verbally in group and one-on-one settings; teach and train the folks responsible for upholding policies about how to minimize bias; and institute a set of checks and balances geared toward making sure they are evenly applied.

DEFINING POLICY

A policy is a defined set of principles that guide decisions and outcomes inside of an organization. Some of the policies organizations put in place are legally mandated, and others are strongly encouraged, recommended, or asked for by employees, customers, partners, and other key stakeholders.

Generally, when I say "policy" to my clients, they jump to the standard employee handbook policies, which include everything from equal opportunity, work schedule, health and safety, benefits, and anti-harassment. You can see how some of these, in theory, would keep employees safe. Engaging in equal opportunity employment prevents discrimination based on social identity status and anti-harassment is meant to both discourage workplace harassment and create channels for eliminating unwanted behaviors. While many of the policies in a standard employee handbook protect employees, in my experience, still more protect the company. There is nothing wrong with protecting the company, but when fostering a culture of belonging built on the safety of marginalized groups, it's important to center attention on your employees.

As you are defining your policies, you can hold yourself accountable to that intention by asking:

- Who are these policies designed to protect?[4]

- How can I involve the people this is designed to protect in the process of defining this policy?
- How will we as an organization uphold these policies?

There are dozens of policies you may choose to include in your employee handbook. As you are determining what to include, think and look expansively about what you might need to spell out, either to be clear or hold others accountable. One practice I adopted in my own company that has served me well is to consider my employees' workplace rights and capture them transparently, clearly, and openly. I often check what I have proposed or put together using fact sheets from Women Employed, an advocacy organization dedicated to advancing the rights of working women. By seeing how they break down issues like family and medical leave, healthcare coverage for caretakers, paid sick days, and sexual harassment from the perspective of the worker, I can hold myself accountable to a higher standard.

When we are auditing client organizations, we note which policies show up frequently, and which ones don't, as well as how they are worded. This also applies to how we evaluate the types of leave offered. For example, do adoptive parents, foster parents, or other caregivers receive the same parental leave? We have noticed that many of our clients don't have formal antiharassment policies. We pay special attention to this gap because we know the numbers around just one subset of harassment: 60 percent of women report "unwanted sexual attention, sexual coercion, sexually crude conduct, or sexist comments" in the workplace, 90 percent of employees who experience harassment never file a formal complaint, and 75 percent never informally complain to their employers.[5] One of our organizations did have an antiharassment policy, but the language indicated that engaging in harassment led to an "unprofessional environment that decreased productivity" without mentioning the rights or experiences of those on the receiving end of harassment. "We care about harassment because it interrupts your workday" set a tone within the organization that what mattered above all else was the work product, not the safety of employees.

It's my opinion that this kind of policy framing would have been caught if more folks had been involved in developing it. And when I say more folks, I mean a lot more.

One of the practices I advocate for within organizations is living documents, especially codes of conduct and employee handbooks. The way they work is relatively straightforward. Essentially, a living employee handbook is one that employees can suggest changes and edits to, like a wiki or Google Doc, subject to HR and leadership approval. If done well, with the appropriate presentation across multiple channels, periodic reminders, and modeling from folks within the organization, this document engages employees more meaningfully in protection, promotes thinking and discussion around company policies, and creates social accountability. To put together a living employee handbook:

- Finalize any edits, changes, or additions to your existing employee handbook to ensure folks are reacting to the most complete version you can offer.
- Decide on who the final "approvers" of suggestions will be, and also at what cadence the suggested changes will be reviewed (monthly, quarterly, annually).
- Upload the document to an editable or suggestion-friendly platform.
- Promote to team members, especially through all-hands and team meetings, with an emphasis that it's suggestion-friendly and you want them to influence its development.
- Collect suggestions and review before making decisions about whether to incorporate.
- Incorporate changes, saving the version history, and share with the company what was incorporated and what wasn't, with reasons in each case.

TRANS-INCLUSIVE BENEFITS

Compensation, benefits, and leave are all critical components of protection-based policies. They also directly relate to social identity. In their research on health insurance coverage, The Human Rights Campaign found that health insurance plans generally discriminate against transgender employees.[6] To measure how inclusive your plan is for transgender and gender nonconforming employees, consider the following.[7]

- *The health insurance plan affirms coverage.* A successful protection strategy is one where the company health insurance plan provides coverage for employees that is not subject to transgender exclusion. For example, many plans cover hysterectomies as surgical procedures, but exclude coverage if the purpose of the hysterectomy is gender affirmation surgery. A trans-inclusive plan removes or modifies any trans exclusions related to care for hormone therapies, mental health counseling, surgical procedures, medical visits, and lab procedures.[8]
- *The health insurance plan documentation is made available and accessible to employees, and clearly communicates trans inclusive benefits for employees and their dependents.* The plan should clearly state what the coverage for trans employees and their dependents is, and it should be provided to them without them having to ask.
- *The health insurance plan covers the World Professional Association for Transgender Health's Standards of Care (SOC)'s list of procedures.* By understanding their guide on "Standards of Care for the Health of Transsexual, Transgender, and Gender Nonconforming People," you can gauge how inclusive your existing plan is. From there, you can request modifications and changes if you

find not all of the procedures included in the SOC's guide are covered.[9]

- *The health insurance plan isn't restricted.* Coverage should not be capped at a certain amount, either at the lifetime or annual levels. Many plans set dollar maximums, so checking on this is important to make sure care is in fact accessible for trans and gender nonconforming employees.

- *Your organization supports short-term leave related to trans-inclusive procedures.* You should have a clearly articulated leave policy around your trans-inclusive procedures that states leave term, costs covered, and guidelines for reporting and taking leave. These should be presented to and discussed with employees without them having to ask.

It's worth noting that these guidelines are specific to gender transition and affirmation, but trans-inclusive policies go beyond these kinds of care. As you organize your parental leave and family and medical leave policies, other areas to consider are:

- Benefits around alternative family planning (i.e. IUI, IVF, adoption, and surrogacy).
- Coverage for dependents in same sex domestic partnerships.
- Parental leave options for birth/non-birth parents.

As you are planning out your benefits and policies to support and protect your employees, you may consider hiring a consultant that specializes in creating inclusive environments for trans and gender-nonconforming employees.

PROCESSES

The processes that allow for the full realization of protection, at least in my estimation, are the restorative ones. If well-constructed, policies lay out the processes necessary to uphold them. But beware: despite the most considered policies, breaches of trust and trauma[10] will still occur at the micro and macro level. Essentially, to err is human, and we are collectively embedded in environments shaped by larger social forces that will take a long time to redefine or abolish. That's why when I teach and implement protection strategies in our client organizations, I focus on the processes that help support recovery and healing.

The principle that most supports my philosophy on the role of restorative dialogue and behaviors inside workplaces comes from the poet Natasha Trethewey's memoir about her own experiences with trauma: "To survive trauma, one must be able to tell a story about it." It's no surprise, then, that there has been an explosion of "Courageous Conversations about Race," "Brave Spaces," and story-listening activities inside companies across industries and sizes. Employees understand the inherent value of creating spaces to listen to and share stories. Yet, depending on the context, environment, and participants, these experiences can either fall flat, or worse, perpetuate harm. These potentially negative outcomes depend on how power dynamics are named and addressed, what pressures certain people feel, for what purposes these groups come together, and to what extent people are willing to be vulnerable and open to listening, rather than committing themselves to convincing others and being right. For this reason, I gravitate toward restorative processes rooted in healing-centered engagement in my own practice.

HEALING-CENTERED ENGAGEMENT

Shawn Ginwright, Associate Professor of Education and African American Studies at San Francisco State University and the author of *Hope and Healing in Urban Education: How Urban Activists and Teachers are Reclaiming Matters of the Heart*, coined the term "healing-centered engagement" as an alternative to trauma-informed care when considering how to best support youth who had experienced trauma. His theory of healing has greatly influenced many DEIB practitioners and social justice advocates, myself included.

His advocacy for shifting the conversation from trauma to healing comes from a place of believing a term like "trauma-informed care" privileges the clinical over the political and pathologizes the people it is meant to support. Yet, "a healing-centered approach views trauma not simply as an individual isolated experience, but rather highlights the ways in which trauma and healing are experienced collectively. The term healing-centered engagement expands how we think about responses to trauma and offers a more holistic approach to fostering well-being."[11]

One of the most applicable principles from Ginwright's models at work, rather than youth development, is that healing-centered engagement should be culturally grounded and viewed as tied to restoring identity. The term "healing circle," which is becoming more widely adopted in corporate settings, helps illustrate what this principle looks like in practice. As Ginwright points out, indigenous cultures use a healing circle forum to share stories that help them connect to their ancestors and traditions. The analog in facilitated workplace environments is *caucused* healing circles. Essentially, members group together by social identity types (such as BIPOC and White or cisgender and transgender) and have a discussion about healing within the context of their identities.

The healing circle format reinforces another important principle: healing-centered engagement is strengths-based and more focused on the well-being we want than symptoms we want to treat. While these circles give people the opportunity to name and discuss harm experienced, this is not their primary intention. Instead, they recognize that viewing people as "the worst thing that happened to them" is limiting and superficial. They opt to focus on what the participants want to achieve moving forward, rather than stopping at treating the symptoms of harm from the past.

Committing to in healing-centered engagement as an ongoing process can feel intimidating. For this reason, keeping in mind some of the practices encouraged in the overall philosophy is so valuable; you aren't working from a blank page, but a method that's established and tested. The ones that most resonate for the employees in our client organizations are:

- *Build empathy.* Story-sharing, whether informally or in structured settings, helps create shared understanding and emotional connection. But someone has to be vulnerable first. At Ethos, we ask our facilitators to be the most vulnerable people in the room to mitigate the emotional risk of story-sharing by leading with their own stories. A similar approach might apply to leaders within your teams or the broader organization.
- *Foreground possibilities.* Healing-centered engagement hinges on the idea that people have the agency to envision who they want to be and realize that in the real world. Whether through team-building exercises, coaching, facilitated discussions, or even prompts for individual reflection, encourage employees to design their lives.
- *Reflect and encourage action.* Promote a culture of reflection, asking those engaging in this process to consider what healing might mean for them. As my friend and self-care expert Taylor Elyse Morrison often says, self-care is "listening within and responding in the most loving way possible." Once they have landed on their response, encourage them to take action and support them in what they plan, whether it's organizing access to resources, calling for change, or otherwise. As Ginwright points out, "Research has demonstrated that

building this sense of power and control among traumatized groups is perhaps one of the most significant features in restoring holistic well-being."

A blueprint for how to lead a healing circle can be found at: http://www.alidamirandawolff.com/bookreaders.

PRACTICES

When it comes to the realm of protection, the expectation from folks within organizations is that this is the work HR and compliance professionals do. But this ignores the fact that safety in the workplace is largely defined by person-to-person and intrateam experiences. Managers, peers, direct reports, customers, and even vendors are all part of the pantheon of relationships a single employee will cultivate; and setting up repeatable practices for them is essential to achieving a healthy environment. There are many practices that folks might engage with, but for our purposes, I want to look at the two most universal for all members of an organization: awkward conversations and apologies.

AWKWARD CONVERSATIONS

There is value in awkwardness. If you subscribe to Melissa Dahl's definition of awkwardness as that moment of awareness when you realize that someone does not see you the same way you see yourself, then you know awkwardness can bring incredible insights and personal growth. The problem, of course, is that no one wants to feel cringeworthy. It comes with the sting of potential social rejection, judgment, ridicule, and scorn. As social creatures, most people want to avoid those feelings as much as possible; being liked, accepted, and welcomed is part of feeling safe. We are often afraid to compromise that safety, even in the face of important conversations, like those about race, disability, gender identity, or queer identity.

But while everyone can feel awkward, those in dominant groups often have the privilege of choosing to experience it less. If we want to protect the people within our organizations most likely to experience acts of bias and discrimination, start with teaching people how to tolerate the discomfort of awkwardness. While this can certainly happen in healing circles and other facilitated sessions, the reality is that people go to work to complete a set of responsibilities that are typically outside of these more structured environments. You have to bake these kinds of skills and practices into what they do every day.

On my team, that means finding new and different ways to reframe our relationships to comfort. This is a place where COCo's work on the characteristics of white supremacy culture provides an invaluable tool. In their definition of "right to comfort" as a characteristic, they point out that people with power feel they have a right to emotional and psychological comfort that often goes hand-in-hand with a series of problematic behaviors including valuing "logic" over "emotion" and calling out or ostracizing people who cause discomfort.[12]

For us, to challenge the idea of comfort as both a given and something universally positive, we remember race scholar Beverly Tatum's admission, "Every conversation that has changed my life is one I did not want to have." We talk regularly about the possibility that comes from awkwardness and discomfort, and we engage in daily actions that help us lean into it. This includes:

- Routinely talking about our biases, especially in the hiring process, and asking for the group to hold us accountable to them.
- Sharing our mistakes around social identity and what led to them (such as when I unintentionally used an ableist term while talking to a disability activist).

- Meeting about and having discussions around potentially "awkward" conversations ("How is the team reacting to the shooting in Atlanta? And how should we respond?").
- Engaging in round robins to make sure everyone participates in awkward conversations, even if it's more comfortable for them to let others do the talking.
- Sharing organizational feedback as a full team, including on how the facilitators supported their audiences and where they had limitations.

Most of all, in our embracing of awkwardness, we are acknowledging that there is a kind of safety on the team. Shunning someone for being awkward or breaking decorum would raise more issues than creating space for those behaviors.

THE ART OF THE APOLOGY

Just as Daniel Coyle found that organizations where people say "thank you" often have healthier cultures, I have found that those where employees say "I apologize" are more inclusive and equitable.

In my favorite film of 2020, Emerald Fennell's intense #MeToo-revenge story, *Promising Young Woman*, a young woman, Cassie, seeks vengeance on those who she deems responsible for the rape and subsequent suicide of her best friend Nina. Person by person, she asks these people to acknowledge what happened and apologize. When they don't apologize or make excuses related to not wanting to ruin the life of a "promising young man" or "being just kids at the time" or even blaming Nina for drinking, our protagonist enacts various forms of punishment. Except, in one case. Cassie arrives on the doorstep of the lawyer who bullied Nina into dropping her case against her abuser, earnest in her assertion that today would be his day of reckoning. In their conversation, the lawyer remembers Nina, acknowledges the harm he committed against her and others like her, names the incentives that benefited him as a result of committing that harm, apologizes, and asks for forgiveness. This moment marks a major shift in the plot; Cassie forgives him. He can't undo the past, but he can acknowledge it was real, that Nina mattered, and that he was wrong.

This particular encounter strikes me because if others had apologized, this would have been a very different film, one about a grieving woman grappling with a broken system and a culture of violence toward women, but who ultimately comes to terms with her loss. Instead, every other person is defensive, recalcitrant, and unwilling to make amends. And so, the film turns chilling and violent, in the typical way of revenge movies. While this extreme example doesn't apply exactly to workplaces, the idea of a person or group of people refusing to admit harm is a standard day-to-day behavior. There are so many reasons why: a disconnect between how people perceive themselves and how others perceive them, fear of retribution or punishment, denial and shame, a need to keep up appearances, and a clinging to individual goals over group ones. But what if we learned, collectively, to apologize at work? What kind of impact would that have?

The answer at one client organization was transformation. After hearing a litany of examples of past harm experienced by folks from marginalized groups, a tearful participant volunteered a question that fundamentally shifted the orientation of the room. "What if we just . . . apologized?" For those who had experienced the harm, including open acts of discrimination and harassment, the suggestion struck an emotionally resonant chord. After all this time, what they wanted was an apology, not just from the people who had harmed them, but from those who had stood by and let it happen. One by one, inside and outside of the session, people apologized. And finally, healing really did take place. To be seen and validated, to have others name the injustice and their part in it—that was what those who had been harmed needed to achieve closure. In addition to the apologies, the organization collectively agreed to change its structures to prevent this kind of harm from happening again.

I do not advocate for insincere apologies, but instead, a willingness to own a mistake, a bad day, a gap in knowledge, or even an interpersonal problem. This is why so much of the education around upstander intervention and microaggressions is important, as well as the policies and processes described earlier in this chapter. So, what makes for a good apology?

- Speak in "I" statements.
- Acknowledge what you did, clearly and concisely.
- Apologize for your actions.
- Offer an example of how you might change or be different next time.

Notice what's *not* in this formulation: justification, long-winded explanations, defensiveness, or a focus on what the other person did. It's short and pointed.

It's my experience that people want to apologize but are afraid for a lot of the reasons listed above, as well as a fear of worsening the situation by saying the wrong thing while apologizing. For this reason, I recommend making apologies into a part of the culture and modeling the behaviors through people in positions of power first.

Forgiving does not mean forgetting. As I wrote in collaboration with my team in response to the murder of George Floyd in May of 2020, "for those calling for healing and reconciliation, we stand with you but warn against using these words as a means of erasing and forgetting."

Healing and reconciliation *are* the way forward, but the decision for them must come from those impacted. In my practice of reaching toward DEIB, I increasingly understand that I have to shed some of the anguish and anger to make space for the optimism, hope, and joy that make fortitude in this work possible.

ON PERSONAL FLOURISHING

There is a reason I am choosing to end on protection. I know that we must feel safe in order to pursue optimism, at least in some small way. Safety, after all, is our most basic need. And the truth is that while writing this book, when I felt stuck, I was coming from a place of fear. Zadie Smith writes in *Intimations* that "Talking to yourself can be useful. And writing means being overheard." I took these words to heart as I was writing. In many ways, you are overhearing my conversations with myself during a particularly fraught time.

I wrote this book in 2020. During the process I confronted grief personally, professionally, culturally, and nationally. At every stage, I questioned why I omitted one model and added in another, wondered how I was going to write this book in less than 600 pages, and tormented myself with the recurring thought that perhaps this wasn't my book to write at all. I attacked my own identities, got lost in the technical details of how to make changes, and wrote and rewrote the same principles over and over again.

I hit a low point one morning where, in an effort to get my mind off a particularly challenging equity situation at a client company, I watched one of my favorite YouTubers, Abigail Thorn (also known as Philosophy Tube), tackle the philosophy of work in a video essay about the five jobs she had held in her life. In the process of watching the video, my chest seized, and I found myself in a spiral: work as we know it is broken, there are no real solutions that tangibly improve lives, the only answer is to abolish work altogether, and so far no one knows how to abolish work without ruining billions of lives. This led me to question my role as a business owner, a worker, and someone who dedicates her life to the improvement of working conditions for underrepresented and underserved groups. Maybe that life purpose is not just aspirational, but misguided and impossible, I thought.

Fortunately, I had a prescheduled call with a friend who has been advocating for underrepresented and underserved groups for longer than I have been alive. I walked her through my existential spiral, emphasizing my feelings of hopelessness and helplessness. Calmly, she reminded me that there may be a lot of issues with work as it stands today, but it's the system we have. And since there isn't a new system birthing itself overnight, we have a responsibility to work with this one. "Why do we care about representation in leadership if the whole system is rotten?" she started. "Because, if we bring in new voices that haven't held positions with power before, there is a stronger possibility that priorities and norms can change. We have the chance to work with the current structures as part of a spectrum of efforts to transform them."

For the first time in a long time, I felt hopeful.

My friend's words brought me back to a poem from Prageeta Sharma's *Grief Sequence*, a collection of poems about the experience of mourning her husband's death. "Closure isn't closure but openings."[13]

In writing this book, one of my goals has been to encourage you to imagine a better future, one that promotes your own personal flourishing, as well as the flourishing of others. Only through collective thriving can we make change sustainable and whole. As you take the ideas from this book into your daily life, I hope you will ask yourself:

- What does it mean to build a better future?
- How will you define what that is?
- What are the possibilities?
- Where do you hold hope and optimism?
- What steps might you take to realize that future?
- Who will you bring with you on the journey?

Today is an opening. Make new possibilities.

ACKNOWLEDGMENTS

I have wanted to be a writer since I was in preschool and imagining my career as a famous artist supermodel balancing humanitarian acts of service with finding the time to promote my bestselling novels. Throughout my life, this dream of being a published author has seemed out of reach. In the months I've spent writing this book, I have found myself overwhelmed and in awe of the fact that I am writing a book, and that my dream has become a reality. There are many people who made this possible and not enough pages to write about all of them. My gratitude for them is immeasurable and indescribable.

It turns out for me that writing the book proposal and finding it the right home was harder than writing the book. I want to thank Jessica Zweig for telling me there was a book in me in the first place, and reminding me to keep trying, even in the face of rejection. Rea Frey was an invaluable reader in the book proposal phase, and without her, I would never have found an agent. My agent, Marilyn Allen, advocated for this book, even during a time when publishers were skeptical anyone would buy a book about diversity, equity, inclusion, and belonging.

I want to thank everyone at the HarperCollins Leadership team for standing behind me as a first-time author, and supporting the development, editing, and promotion of this book. In particular, I owe a great deal to my editor, Tim Burgard, who I knew from our first meeting together would understand my goals for publishing this book.

I cannot understate the enormous importance of my readers in developing the version of the book you see now. Michael Winnick, whose partnership as a client and collaborator fundamentally shaped my business, was a generous sounding board who challenged me to make the book more reader-centric, add more stories and examples, and strip out dry language. Without you, this book would be a lot more boring. Tiff Voltz, who has been a friend, cheerleader, and brainstorm partner for years, brought compassion, discernment, and frankly *bomb* line edits to my manuscript. She also reminded me to bring in humanity and warmth when I got too into the nuts and bolts of the process. Finally, Amanda Paul is perhaps the highest achieving and most self-aware fellow DEIB practitioner I have partnered with, and I owe her for checking my biases. She was diligent in rooting out ableist language, identifying hard to understand language, and reminding me to present multiple options for people living through different experiences in their companies.

I would be remiss if I didn't recognize the Ethos team, both current and previous members, for constantly supporting me in writing this book, even when we were literally doubling and tripling in size and *any* extra time from me would have been a lifesaver. Strother Gaines, Sonni Conway, Pondharshini Sadasivam, Amalia Loiseau, Jake Burger, Walter Faro, Britney Robertson, Michelle Bess, Trevor Jenkins, LaTonya Wilkins, Kirsten Ramos, Khalilah Lyons, and Francine Bailey, thank you, truly.

There are two Ethosians I specifically want to acknowledge. Lisa Tomiko Blackburn has been a partner at Ethos so that I can be an author of this book; they reminded me to make time for the creative process even when I couldn't give myself that same grace. And of course, I owe special thanks to Lexi Brown for always thinking of how to get this book into people's hands. It's so special to be with you on this journey to launch.

To all those practitioners of social justice, DEIB and culture who helped shape my experiences and thinking, thank you. Special credit goes to the extraordinary minds and activist hearts of Sukari Pinnock Fitts, adrienne maree brown, Abigail Thorn, Alice Wong, Derald Wing Sue, Cathy Park Hong, Guerrilla Girls, Mia Birdsong, and Natalie Wynn.

This book is a tribute to my clients. Many of these stories came from our shared experiences, and it was with your challenges and opportunities in mind that I drew inspiration for each and every chapter. You are all so special to me. I have sent you all notes of appreciation and gifts in the last year, and I hope you know how important you are to me.

Because there would be no Ethos and no *Cultures of Belonging* without them, I want to call out my first-ever clients at Ethos. To everyone from Buildout for believing in me, my business, and this book, thank you. And, to Buildout's founder, Vishu Ramanathan, thank you for being the person I debated as I navigated gray areas while writing this book, and for inspiring me to believe that change really was possible in tech companies in the first place. To all of the original ladies at SimplyBe. Agency, our growth has been entwined and interconnected, and you are such a huge part of why I do what I do. To the leaders of the Women Influence Chicago Accelerator, especially Julia Kanouse, Aimee Schuster, and Christine Schoeff, thank you for betting on me; the program has changed my life and kept me hopeful even in the hardest of times.

An incredible community of women banded together to form my support system during this pivotal time. My Embolden community, especially my Mastermind group, showered me with emotional support and positivity. Ewa Baska, Gina Contella, Michelle Chen, Pooja Shah, Taylor Morrison, and of course, Tiff Voltz—thank you for listening, and for crowning me with a unicorn wig and scream-singing in Japanese karaoke booths with me until 2:00

a.m. after a truly rough 2019. Without your support, I would have abandoned this book project altogether. My friend and thought partner Dorie Blesoff acted as a confidante when I had nowhere else to turn, and also reminded me, crucially, that this work is not about pathology, scarcity, or deficiency, but simply about asking the question, "What can I contribute?" Yael Shy taught me to treat myself with care and prioritize my own healing while making space for all of the voices and struggles inside me, instead of pushing them down or resisting them. Alison Hirshorn has transformed my life and helped me come to greater clarity on who I am and how to accept myself.

To my best friend, Katina Vradelis, if anyone helped me workshop this book over the years it was coming into being, it was you. Thank you for always being willing to take the opposite perspective, but also letting me know when I am totally right. And, thank you for continuing to be the Ann Perkins to my Leslie Knope, even after ten years.

To Oswald, Napoleon, Penelope, Cassie, and Fergus for being sources of unconditional joy and comfort, especially in the midst of a pandemic, socioeconomic crisis, and extended period of civil and social unrest. Thank you for giving me hope for a better future.

Thank you to my mom for encouraging me to pursue reading and writing from the moment I could until now; my appetite for learning and appreciation for books comes from you. I love you.

Finally, last but not least, thank you to my husband, Isaac Larkin, who is so involved in my work that he is an unofficial member of my team and who, even in this moment, is showing his support by bringing dinner up to me in my office. You have always said "hell yes" to my dreams before I have, and so, they come true.

NOTES

INTRODUCTION

1. Rachel Botsman, *Who Can You Trust? How Technology Brought Us Together and Why It Might Drive Us Apart* (New York: Public Affairs, 2017).

2. adrienne maree brown, *Emergent Strategy: Shaping Change, Changing Worlds* (AK Press, 2017).

3. This is definitely not Nassim Taleb's intention for his book or his explanation of this phenomenon; it's just how my mind interpreted his research.

CHAPTER ONE

1. "The 2017 Tech Leavers Study," Kapor Center, 2017, https://www.kapor center.org/tech-leavers/.

2. Joshua Rothman, "The Meaning of 'Culture,'" The *New Yorker,* December 26, 2014, https://www.newyorker.com/books/joshua-rothman/meaning -culture.

3. Simon Sinek, *Leaders Eat Last: Why Some Teams Pull Together and Others Don't* (Portfolio: 2014).

4. Nancy DiTomaso and George G. Gordon, "Predicting Corporate Performance from Organizational Culture," *Journal of Management Studies* 29, no. 6 (November 1992), 783–798, https://doi.org/10.1111/j.1467-6486.1992 .tb00689.x.

5. "'Give Away Your Legos' and Other Commandments for Scaling Startups," *First Round Review,* September 10, 2015, https://firstround.com/review /give-away-your-legos-and-other-commandments-for-scaling-startups/.

6. Dan Denison and Aneil K. Mishra, "Toward a Theory of Organizational Culture and Effectiveness," *Organization Science* 6, no. 2 (April 1995), 204– 223, https://doi.org/10.1287/orsc.6.2.204.

7. "Managing Employee Turnover," PayScale, December 22, 2017, http:// www.payscale.com/compensation-today/2017/12/managing-employee -turnover.

8. I am using the term "token" to refer to the phenomenon where organizations hire, platform, and highlight the few people from marginalized groups in their organization to demonstrate their diversity, equity, inclusion, and belonging.

9. "Where Is the Diversity in Publishing? The 2019 Diversity Baseline Survey Results," Lee & Low Books, January 28, 2020, https://blog.leeandlow .com/2020/01/28/2019diversitybaselinesurvey/.

10. At Ethos, we added three additional identities, "Tribal/Indigenous Status" to call out a group we often see left out in discussions of race and ethnicity, "Body Type and Size" based on groundbreaking work by writers and activists like Roxanne Gay, and "Caretaker Status" to acknowledge anyone responsible for the unpaid primary care of another person, whether a child, loved one, or family member.

11. It's important to note that for the sake of simplicity, we have adopted a binary of "dominant" versus "marginalized" that doesn't directly comment on the spectra that exist for each social identity category. The spectrum matters, though. Being able to "pass" as the dominant group gives those in the marginalized group more access than those who cannot. Similarly, being considered to be farther away from the dominant group also leads to higher levels of disempowerment. While women are marginalized in the workplace, transgender women experience far greater rates of workplace discrimination.

12. "The Wellbeing Effect of Education," UKRI Economic and Social Council, July 2014, https://esrc.ukri.org/news-events-and-publications/evidence-briefings/the-wellbeing-effect-of-education/.

CHAPTER TWO

1. In this case, "progressive" refers to willing to try new things in an organization, while "conservative" means married to the status quo. It's amazing to me how many tech companies talk about new ideas, like consensus-based decision-making and holacracy, but are absolutely devoted to standard management practices from the 1980s, including command-and-control leadership and compartmentalization. They are also the most likely companies in our portfolio to focus on color blindness as a best practice rather than a common form of microaggression. It goes without saying that this framing does not apply to *all* tech companies, but I've been impressed with the sheer volume where this is the case.

2. Jemima McEvoy, "Every CEO And Leader That Stepped Down Since Black Lives Matter Protests Began," *Forbes*, July 1, 2020, https://www.forbes.com/sites/jemimamcevoy/2020/07/01/every-ceo-and-leader-that-stepped-down-since-black-lives-matter-protests-began/.

3. Don Share, "Editor's Note," Poetry Foundation, July 2020, https://www.poetryfoundation.org/poetrymagazine/articles/153943/editor39s-note-5f0f1bc747964.

4. Mapping Police Violence, November 2020, https://mappingpoliceviolence.org/.

5. Ibid.

6. "Herstory," Black Lives Matter, September 7, 2019, https://blacklivesmatter.com/herstory/.

7. Gita Jackson, "We're All Living In The Cool Zone Now," *VICE*, June 2, 2020, http://www.vice.com/en/article/pkypdg/were-all-living-in-the-cool-zone-now.

8. Maria Godoy and Daniel Wood, "What Do Coronavirus Racial Disparities Look Like State By State?" NPR, May 30, 2020, http://www.npr.org/sections/health-shots/2020/05/30/865413079/what-do-coronavirus-racial-disparities-look-like-state-by-state.

9. Vernā Myers, "How to Overcome Our Biases? Walk Boldly Toward Them," TED talk, November 2014, http://www.ted.com/talks/verna_myers_how _to_overcome_our_biases_walk_boldly_toward_them.

10. Catherine Powell, "The Color and Gender of COVID: Essential Workers, Not Disposable People: Think Global Health," Council on Foreign Relations, June 2020, http://www.thinkglobalhealth.org/article/color-and -gender-covid-essential-workers-not-disposable-people.

11. Rodney Foxworth, "Government Programs Are Shortchanging Minority-Owned Small Businesses," The World News, May 2020, https://theworldnews .net/us-news/government-programs-are-shortchanging-minority-owned -small-businesses-dafs-can-help.

12. Isabel Wilkerson, "Where Do We Go From Here?" in The Fire This Time: A New Generation Speaks About Race (New York: Charles Scribner's Sons, 2016).

13. Frederick A. Miller and Judith H. Katz, "The Path from Exclusive Club to Inclusive Organization," The Kaleel Jamison Consulting Group, 2007, https://copdei.extension.org/wp-content/uploads/2019/06/The-Path -from-Exclusive-Club.pdf.

14. These bullet points are largely informed by the work of Nathaniel Popper in "'Tokenized': Inside Black Workers' Struggles at the King of Crypto Start-Ups" for The New York Times, November 27, 2020, blended with private accounts shared with me from several former Coinbase employees.

15. Brian Armstrong, "Coinbase Is a Mission Focused Company," The Coinbase Blog, September 8, 2020, https://blog.coinbase.com/coinbase-is-a-mission -focused-company-af882df8804.

16. Brian Armstrong, "A Follow up to Coinbase as a Mission Focused Company," The Coinbase Blog, October 8, 2020, https://blog.coinbase.com/a -follow-up-to-coinbase-as-a-mission-focused-company-6e7545e9aea2.

17. Frederick A. Miller and Judith H. Katz, "The Path from Exclusive Club to Inclusive Organization."

18. In both of his public letters, Armstrong emphasizes that in order to achieve the company's mission, team members can't become distracted by trying to do too many things. He suggests that employees were asking Coinbase to become a social justice organization. Based on what I've seen and heard from employee reports, the majority of employees did not ask for Coinbase to focus on the outside world, but to change internal policies and behaviors when it came to underrepresented and underserved groups.

19. Pro Tip: Use the social identity key in chapter one as a guide for your team members.

CHAPTER THREE

1. My clients always challenge this point by saying, "But what if those employees are underperforming? What if they want to shape inclusion so that no one does any work and harbors ill will toward the company?" My response is always the same: "Why are these people still working at your organization?"

2. Chana Joffe-Walt's five-part series, "Nice White Parents," explores gentrification and integration in New York public schools. The challenges Joffe-Walt reports on remind me of the ones I see inside of workplaces. Throughout the episodes, there are clashes between White parents and BIPOC parents. White

parents focus on hosting fundraisers, launching community service initiatives, and drafting statements and charters, while BIPOC parents push for smaller classroom sizes, access to better learning materials, and safer schools. The latter's goals seemed less exciting to White parents. After all, the White kids experienced far less underresourcing than BIPOC kids did. I see the same dynamic play out in workplaces. On the DEIB committees we support, I notice a push and pull between allies who want to see "bigger and better" changes, and underrepresented folks asking for basic rights and experiences they are being denied. The latter group is critiqued for thinking small. They're also the group with the best insight into what the most real needs are.

3. Claude Steele, *Whistling Vivaldi: How Stereotypes Affect Us and What We Can Do* (New York: W. W. Norton & Company, 2011), 77.

4. I don't mean to call out my husband—I use him as an example because he is one of the most accepting people I know and even he falls into the intergroup bias trap.

5. Daniel Coyle, *The Culture Code: The Secrets of Highly Successful Groups* (New York: Bantam, 2018), 8.

6. One example forever stands out to me. I conducted over twenty research interviews at a client organization where almost every participant mentioned not having transparent salary information, which contributed to a culture of opacity and perceived discrimination. In going through the artifact review, I found salary bands that were openly presented in the general wiki. I also found a recording of a meeting where they were presented and their People Operations leader invited questions and one-on-one follow-ups. In looking at when the meeting took place and the levels were created, I realized many of the folks who told me that pay was opaque and bands didn't exist had joined after the wiki page was created and the meeting was held. They hadn't been given a tour of the wiki, and their managers hadn't talked with them about compensation. Needless to say, I had clear recommendations for how to address this gap.

7. A common theme throughout this book will be the importance of getting leadership on board before any promises are made to employees. If there is one thing I strive to avoid in organizations, it's making promises I can't keep to the people I am most trying to support. If I promise we will make all decisions based on consensus from now on, but privately a CEO tells me it's not going to happen, where does that leave expectations, trust, and orientation toward the organization for the greater team?

CHAPTER FOUR

1. "The State of the Gender Pay Gap 2020," PayScale, accessed January 25, 2021, http://www.payscale.com/data/gender-pay-gap. Please note that the 81 cent figure shows the uncontrolled gender pay gap, which takes the ratio of the median earnings of women to men without controlling for various compensable factors, including other social identity markers.

2. Mia Birdsong, *How We Show Up: Reclaiming Family, Friendship, and Community* (New York: Hachette Go, 2020), 2.

3. If you have any doubts about this, go back to chapter three for a refresher on mindbugs and where they come from.

4. It's worth noting that intersectional issues were at play in this particular dynamic. We both had dominant and marginalized identities. He was racially marginalized while I was racially dominant, but our gender power dynamics were reversed. He pointed this out by saying that "being a woman didn't count as a form of marginalization," which plays into the larger context of those in a dominant group not being aware of marginalized experience.

5. "Discrimination: What It Is, and How to Cope," American Psychological Association, October 2019, https://www.apa.org/topics/discrimination.

6. Acts like this, which perpetuate racism, are a part of the system of racism.

7. "Structural Racism Timeline," ERASE Racism, accessed January 25, 2021, http://www.eraseracismny.org/structural-racism-timeline.

8. I want to extend special thanks to Michael Ciszewski, who, in Georgetown's diversity management program, combined the "I don't like" framework from Rick Maurer's *Beyond the Wall of Resistance* with Frances Frei's logic, empathy, and authenticity model for trust from her TED Talk, "How to Build (and Rebuild) Trust." I am applying that combination here, though with my own analysis.

9. It really wasn't. I am both a literalist and a completionist, and together, these qualities can make for painfully earnest, but misguided, responses.

10. This is an equity practice. You make sure everyone receives the same information (equality) and then you customize its delivery based on individual needs (equity).

11. Wendy S. Walters, "Lonely in America," in *The Fire This Time: A New Generation Speaks About Race.*

12. Kevin L. Nadal, "A Guide to Responding to Microaggressions," *CUNY Forum* 2, no. 1 (2014), 71–72.

13. I want to express enormous thanks to Sukari Pinnock Fitts, who first taught this framework to me in my diversity management program at Georgetown University.

CHAPTER FIVE

1. James N. Baron and Michael T. Hannan. "Organizational Blueprints for Success in High-Tech Start-Ups: Lessons from the Stanford Project on Emerging Companies," *California Management Review* 44, no. 3 (2002).

CHAPTER SIX

1. Gina Belli, "How Many Jobs Are Found Through Networking, Really?" *PayScale*, March 4, 2017, https://www.payscale.com/career-news/2017/04/many-jobs-found-networking.

2. I also learned it from the DEIB practitioner Michelle Bess, who runs the largest Slack-based networking group for DEIB professionals, The Brave Space. Learn more about her work at www.wearethebravespace.com.

3. Signe-Mary McKernan, Caleb Quakenbush, Caroline Ratcliffe, Emma Kalish, and C. Eugene Steuerle, *Nine Charts about Wealth Inequality in America* (updated), October 4, 2017, https://apps.urban.org/features/wealth-inequality-charts/.

4. This list is not meant to be comprehensive; it's a jumping off point for designing your own questions.

5. A common theme throughout *Cultures of Belonging* is to think critically about existing structures and the ways underrepresented and underserved groups may be excluded from decision-making at different points. Try to observe and correct as you find gaps.

6. I recommend Project/Case Study interviews for all roles, regardless of the function or level.

7. These messages should not make it into the Hiring Communications Plan if they are not true! Balancing the current state with the aspirational one is challenging, but know that sooner or later, candidates will find out more about your organization for themselves. If your statements are aspirational, let them know.

8. "Job Seeker Nation Report 2020," Jobvite, September 2, 2020, https://www.jobvite.com/jsn2020/.

9. Gregory Lewis, "This Job Description Heatmap Shows You What Candidates Really Care About (and What They Ignore)," LinkedIn Talent Blog, June 19, 2018, https://business.linkedin.com/talent-solutions/blog/job-descriptions/2018/job-description-heatmap.

10. In 2020, California voted against Proposition 16, which would lift the ban on affirmative action. Despite Zachary Bleemer's comprehensive research on the effects of the affirmative action ban in "Affirmative Action, Mismatch, and Economic Mobility After California's Proposition 209," namely that Black and Latinx students were harmed by the ban and Whites and Asian Americans were not positively impacted, 56 percent of voters voted against lifting the ban, as opposed to 44 percent of voters who voted in support of lifting it. In the wake of the national protests spurred by the murder of George Floyd, the margin, which was notably wider than when the ban was first introduced in 2009, surprised many. The campaign to leave the ban in place emphasized all the reasons why so many Americans, including in businesses, are ambivalent toward affirmative action. Campaigners raised questions about whether affirmative action promotes stereotypes of racial inferiority (people from marginalized groups could only be admitted if higher education institutions had quotas) and hurts overrepresented groups (qualified White and Asian students would miss out on opportunities they rightfully deserved to make space for the "less deserving").

11. Personally, my DiSC assessment has changed three times in the last seven years. My results have depended on how much conflict I was managing, how tired and/or frustrated I was when taking the test, stress level, and how collaborative (or not collaborative) I felt with my team.

12. Upon digging into this assessment, I found coded language throughout that aligned with well-studied categories of microaggressions, including pathologization of communication styles and cultural styles. It's worth noting this person identified as Asian American, and Asian American women are the most likely to be discriminated against for management positions in the US according to PayScale's 2020 report, "The State of the Gender Pay Gap in 2020."

CHAPTER SEVEN

1. Much of this chapter is based in or directly references a blog I wrote in 2018, "The Ultimate Guide to Structuring a 90-Day Onboarding Plan," http://www.alidamirandawolff.com/blog/2018/4/1/the-ultimate-guide -to-structuring-a-90-day-onboarding-plan.
2. "State of the American Workplace," Gallup, November 21, 2020, https:// www.gallup.com/workplace/238085/state-american-workplace-report -2017.aspx.
3. Roy Maurer, "Onboarding Key to Retaining, Engaging Talent." SHRM, August 16, 2015, https://www.shrm.org/resourcesandtools/hr-topics/talent -acquisition/pages/onboarding-key-retaining-engaging-talent.aspx.
4. Jen Dewar, "10 Employee Onboarding Statistics You Must Know in 2021," Sapling HR, August 7, 2020, https://www.saplinghr.com/10-employee -onboarding-statistics-you-must-know-in-2020.
5. Harry G. Frankfurt, *On Bullshit* (Princeton University Press, 2005), 63.

CHAPTER EIGHT

1. Emma Seppälä and Kim Cameron, "Proof That Positive Work Cultures Are More Productive," *Harvard Business Review*, December 1, 2015, https://hbr .org/2015/12/proof-that-positive-work-cultures-are-more-productive.
2. Heather Boushey and Sarah Jane Glynn. "There Are Significant Business Costs to Replacing Employees," Center for American Progress, November 16, 2012, https://www.americanprogress.org/issues/economy/reports /2012/11/16/44464/there-are-significant-business-costs-to-replacing -employees/.
3. Daniel Coyle, *The Culture Code: The Secrets of Highly Successful Groups*, 8.
4. For more on what this means and how to find cultural immersion experiences, read my article on Experiential Learning through Cultural Immersion for *Chief Learning Officer*, https://www.chieflearningofficer.com /2019/01/28/experiential-learning-through-cultural-immersion/.
5. Bruce W. Tuckman, "Developmental Sequence in Small Groups," *Psychological Bulletin* 63, no. 6(1965), 384–399, https://doi.org/10.1037/h0022100.
6. In 1977, Tuckman added a fifth stage called "Adjourning," in which the group recognizes that it's time for the group's work together to end.
7. Leslie Jamison, *The Empathy Exams: Essays* (Minneapolis, Minnesota: Graywolf Press, 2014).
8. This decision to change the name of the technique came from an increasing sense that allies often stood by and served as witnesses, rather than standing up and preventing further harm. We wanted to address this pattern of behavior by asking them to consider themselves differently—not as witnesses, but as proponents and advocates.
9. Patty McCord, *Powerful: Building a Culture of Freedom and Responsibility* (Silicon Guild, 2018), 27.
10. The reality is that in a homogenous Executive Leadership team, leaders may study, practice, and self-educate DEIB two or three times more than their employees and still not have the same level of understanding because they have not experienced the impacts of marginalization first-hand.

Learning concepts and living their effects are not the same; however, learning can help shrink the gap and promote greater empathy that substantially benefits everyone in the organization.

11. This section was largely adapted from my blog, "How to Build Affinity Groups," Alida Miranda-Wolff, "How to Build Affinity Groups," *Medium*, March 4, 2020, https://medium.com/@AlidaMW/how-to-build-affinity -groups-pt-1-b69855d588a.

12. Kim Peters, "Want to Engage Millennial Employees? Prioritize Giving Back," Great Places to Work, November 20, 2019, https://www.greatplace towork.com/resources/blog/engage-millennial-employees.

13. Marcel Mauss, *The Gift: Forms and Functions for Exchange in Archaic Societies* (New York: W. W. Norton & Company, 1954), 77.

CHAPTER NINE

1. "The State of the Gender Pay Gap 2020," PayScale, 2020, https://www .payscale.com/data/gender-pay-gap.

2. "Modern Family Index 2018," Bright Horizons, 2019, https://www.bright horizons.com/-/media/bh-new/newsroom/media-kit/mfi_2018_report _final.ashx.

3. "The State of the Gender Pay Gap 2020."

4. Many organizations have an annual review process for promotion, which typically takes place at the end of the year. That means our Fall Cohort participants often have a greater opportunity to ask for and get a promotion because they are "in cycle."

5. Benjamin Artz, Amanda Gooodall, and Andrew J. Oswald, "Research: Women Ask for Raises as Often as Men, but Are Less Likely to Get Them," *Harvard Business Review*, June 25, 2018, https://hbr.org/2018/06/research -women-ask-for-raises-as-often-as-men-but-are-less-likely-to-get-them.

6. I became an entrepreneur because I understood that I had the capacity to lead departments and teams, but I was met with skepticism so consistently that I decided to say, "Fine, then I'm leaving this system and creating my own." This impulse of leaving to go somewhere else helps explain the real pipeline problem, which as The Kapor Center's Tech Leavers study has shown, occurs mid-career.

7. Anna Wiener, *Uncanny Valley: A Memoir* (MCD, 2020).

8. Mia Birdsong, *How We Show Up*, 42.

9. Vernã A. Myers, *What If I Say the Wrong Thing? 25 Habits for Culturally Effective People* (Chicago: American Bar Association, 2014), 104.

10. Catherine H. Tinsley and Robin J. Ely. "What Most Companies Get Wrong About Men and Women," *Harvard Business Review*, May-June 2018, https://hbr.org/2018/05/what-most-people-get-wrong-about-men-and -women.

11. These questions were adopted from Laszlo Bock's recommendations in *Work Rules.*

12. David G. Smith, Judith E. Rosenstein, and Margaret C. Nikolov. "The Different Words We Use to Describe Male and Female Leaders," *Harvard Business Review*, May 25, 2018, https://hbr.org/2018/05/the-different-words -we-use-to-describe-male-and-female-leaders.

13. As Smith, Rosenstein, and Nikolov highlight in their findings, "Because of widely held societal beliefs about gender roles and leadership, when most people are asked to picture a leader, what they picture is a male leader. Even when women and men behave in leaderly ways among peers—speaking up with new ideas, for example—it's men who are seen as leaders by the group, not women."

14. Shankar Vedantam, "What Does Modern Prejudice Look Like?" NPR, April 22, 2013, https://www.npr.org/sections/codeswitch/2013/04/22/1774 55764/What-Does-Modern-Prejudice-Look-Like.

15. My official position on this issue is that if we achieve equitable workplaces, negotiations won't be necessary because people will be paid equally for equal work, and all jobs will be compensated at or above market. I teach people from marginalized groups to negotiate because our current system requires it; I also let them know that it's not their fault they are paid less, it's our system's. When I teach them, I am managing symptoms. What I am hoping for is a future cure.

16. "Business Succession Planning: Cultivating Enduring Value," Deloitte Development, Deloitte Touche Tohmatsu Limited, 2015, https://www2 .deloitte.com/content/dam/Deloitte/us/Documents/deloitte-private/us -dges-business-succession-planning-collection.pdf.

17. This section was adapted from one of my previous blog posts, Alida Miranda-Wolff, "Managing Conflict on Diverse Teams," Medium, February 5, 2020, https://medium.com/swlh/managing-conflict-on-diverse-teams -1789c6b8a3b7.

18. There will always be some people who rise up regardless of a difficult social environment, but I want us to avoid using edge cases and exceptions to the rule as our measures. We know from more research studies than I care to list in this endnote that people in marginalized groups are held to a higher standard of performance than people in dominant groups, including being expected to overcome adversity and "beat the odds." I think the more relevant question is: Why do the odds need to be against them?

19. Yarrow Dunham, Andrew Scott Baron, and Susan Carey, "Consequences of 'Minimal' Group Affiliations in Children," Child Development 82, no. 3 (March 17, 2011), 793–811, https://doi.org/10.1111/j.1467-8624.2011.01577.x.

20. Jay J. Bavel, Dominic J. Packer, and William A. Cunningham, "The Neural Substrates of In-Group Bias," Psychological Science 19, no. 11 (2008).

21. David Rock, Heidi Grant, and Jacqui Grey, "Diverse Teams Feel Less Comfortable—and That's Why They Perform Better," Harvard Business Review, September 22, 2016, https://hbr.org/2016/09/diverse-teams-feel-less -comfortable-and-thats-why-they-perform-better.

22. Katherine W. Phillips, Katie A. Liljenquist, and Margaret A. Neale, "Is the Pain Worth the Gain? The Advantages and Liabilities of Agreeing With Socially Distinct Newcomers," Personality and Social Psychology Bulletin 35, no. 3 (March 2009), 336–350, https://doi.org/10.1177/0146167208328062.

23. Here's my "practice makes perfect" endnote. It takes thirty days to break a habit, and thirty days to make a new habit. In other words, before getting frustrated with this tool, give it the full sixty days. I still have clients from years ago who say this tool has been the difference between harmony and dysfunction on their teams. That's been the case for me, too.

CHAPTER TEN

1. As with previous comments, this list is not meant to be exhaustive but illustrative.
2. From my vantage point, these specific characteristics also negatively impact people from other marginalized groups, and in many instances people in dominant groups, too.
3. "White Supremacy Culture in Organizations," Dismantling Racism Works adapted by The Centre for Community Organizations, n.d., accessed January 1, 2021, https://coco-net.org/wp-content/uploads/2019/11/Coco -WhiteSupCulture-ENG4.pdf.
4. Occasionally, I will receive push back to these questions from folks who say, "All of our policies protect all of our employees." But, let's think practically about that. Your parental leave policy, for example, is designed to support parents who need to take time away from work to attend to their families. Not every employee in your organization will become a parent. Perhaps more than anywhere else, social identity takes a front seat in your policy development.
5. "Report of the Co-Chairs of the Select Task Force on the Study of Harassment in the Workplace," U.S. Equal Employment Opportunity Commission, June 2016, https://www.eeoc.gov/june-2016-report-co-chairs-select -task-force-study-harassment-workplace.
6. "Transgender Inclusive Healthcare Coverage CEI Resources," HRC Foundation, accessed January 25, 2021, https://www.thehrcfoundation.org /professional-resources/transgender-inclusive-healthcare-coverage-cei -resources.
7. This is by no means a comprehensive list, but rather a starting point.
8. "Transgender Inclusive Healthcare Coverage CEI Resources."
9. "Standards of Care for the Health of Transsexual, Transgender, and Gender Nonconforming People," The World Professional Association for Transgender Health, accessed January 25, 2021.
10. The term *trauma* is often considered extreme in workplace contexts, but it isn't. I define trauma as too much, too soon, too fast, which can characterize many work environments, especially ones experiencing growth and change. And, if 2020 taught us anything, the line between work and home is so blurred as to no longer exist. When different traumas at broad scales impact employees, they come into work with them.
11. Shawn Ginwright, "The Future of Healing: Shifting From Trauma Informed Care to Healing Centered Engagement," *Medium*, December 9, 2020, https://medium.com/@ginwright/the-future-of-healing-shifting-from -trauma-informed-care-to-healing-centered-engagement-634f557ce69c.
12. "White Supremacy Culture in Organizations," Dismantling Racism Works.
13. Prageeta Sharma, "The Moon Has Set: Poetry Obituary," *Grief Sequence* (Wave Books, 2019), 82.

INDEX

ABOUT THE AUTHOR

Alida Miranda-Wolff is the CEO and founder of Ethos, where she helps organizations create the conditions for everyone to thrive at work by helping them and the people inside them understand their relationships with power, how to use their power responsibly, and how to share their power. Alida is also the learning director of the Women Influence Chicago Accelerator, which supports womxn-identifying technologists in advancing their careers, and a founder of the membership organization Embolden, which is focused on developing friendships between womxn. Alida is the recipient of the University of Chicago's Early Career Achievement Award.